GET A (SPIRITUAL) LIFE

Get a (Spiritual) Life
Staying on Track in the Midst of Distractions

KIM WIER

SERVANT PUBLICATIONS
ANN ARBOR, MICHIGAN

Copyright 2003 by Kim Wier
All rights reserved.

Vine Books is an imprint of Servant Publications especially designed to serve evangelical Christians.

Servant Publications—Mission Statement
We are dedicated to publishing books that spread the gospel of Jesus Christ, help Christians to live in accordance with that gospel, promote renewal in the church, and bear witness to Christian unity.

All scripture quotations, unless indicated, are taken from the Holy Bible, New Living Translation, copyright 1996. Used by permission of Tyndale House Publishers, Inc., Wheaton, IL 60189. All rights reserved.

Scripture quotations marked (NIV) are taken from the HOLY BIBLE, NEW INTERNATIONAL VERSION. Copyright 1973, 1978, 1984 by International Bible Society. Used by permission of Zondervan Publishing House. All rights reserved.

Scripture quotations marked (RSV) are from the Revised Standard Version of the Bible, copyrighted 1946, 1952, 1971 by the Division of Christian Education of the National Council of Churches of Christ in the USA. Used by permission.

Servant Publications
P.O. Box 8617
Ann Arbor, MI 48107
www.servantpub.com

Cover design: Alan Furst, Inc., Minneapolis, Minn.

03 04 05 06 10 9 8 7 6 5 4 3 2 1

Printed in the United States of America
ISBN 1-56955-371-8

Library of Congress Cataloging-in-Publication Data

Wier, Kim.
  Get a (spiritual) life : staying on track in the midst of distractions / Kim Wier.
    p. cm.
  ISBN 1-56955-371-8
  1. Christian women--Religious life. I. Title: Get a life. II. Title.
BV4527.W53 2003
248.8'43--dc21

2003003994

Beyond a relationship with Jesus Christ,
Women only need three things to succeed:
Chocolate, laughter, and girlfriends.
*(Men, of course, only need one thing:
A women who has plenty of the above.)*

This book is dedicated to the amazing women who
have shared with me "In case of emergency only"
chocolate–without regard to zits or cellulite,
laughter that only chicks really get–
even when accompanied by tears,
And unconditional friendship that humbles me.

For
Becky, Gaye, Tommy, Michelle, Pam,
June, Tammi, Linda, Hannah, Winifred

Each a precious gift.

Contents

Welcome to the Real World		9
Day 1:	Starve a Fever	19
Day 2:	I Once Was Lost ...	24
Day 3:	The Fine Print	29
Day 4:	Murder She Wrote	34
Day 5:	All Thumbs	39
Day 6:	Dallas Dolls	44
Day 7:	Birds of a Feather	49
Day 8:	Weenies Rule	54
Day 9:	IOU and UO Him	59
Day 10:	This Little Piggy Stayed Home	64
Day 11:	To Have and to Hold	69
Day 12:	Lost and Found	74
Day 13:	Running on Empty	79
Day 14:	Roll Again	84
Day 15:	Pilot to Co-Pilot	89
Day 16:	Too Many Variables	94
Day 17:	Who Me?	99
Day 18:	While You Were Sleeping	104
Day 19:	Hitch a Ride	109
Day 20:	To Your Battle Stations	114
Day 21:	Wanted	119
Day 22:	Throw Away the Key	124
Day 23:	Strange Bedfellows	129
Day 24:	No Hablo Español	134
Day 25:	Cajun Country	139
Day 26:	Mint Julep, Anyone?	145

Get a (Spiritual) Life

Day 27:	Cry Me a River	150
Day 28:	Hold, Please	155
Day 29:	The Greatest Story Never Told	160
Day 30:	Who's on First?	165
Day 31:	Penalty for Early Withdrawal	170
Tomorrow Is Another Day		175

Welcome to the Real World

Wouldn't you love to meet the guy who first had the idea for a garage sale? Did this maverick know that charging money for chipped pottery and half empty perfume bottles would one day become a national phenomenon, and what did his neighbors think?

If he had been able to foretell the future of his idea, I'm sure he would have patented the concept. All of America might be paying him five cents on every garage sale dollar. Fortunately, he lacked foresight, so today you and I can keep every dime of profit. Of course, truth be told, no amount of money can really make up for all the losses we suffer, preparing to unload our stuff on strangers.

First, there is the loss of time. To have a decent garage sale you must clean out every closet, cabinet, drawer, storage shed, attic, basement, wardrobe, desk, file cabinet, medicine chest, pantry, bookshelf, vanity, bathroom sink, kitchen sink, tool box, glove box, sand box, toy box, box of shoes, shoe tree, and tree house. Nothing is too sacred or too worthless to be included. A respectable sale demands no less than a month of your life. And if you ever plan to have another one, it could take even more. That's because word travels fast through the garage sale network. There are some folks whose yearly cast-offs are so widely reputed that crowds actually mark their calendars in anticipation of the event. On the other hand, if your garage sale consists of the sum total of your broken recliner, half a tube of toothpaste, and 1972 back issues of *National Geographic* magazine, your reputation will suffer. The only person who will ever come to your future sales is your mother-in-law, just to make sure you don't try to sell the ceramic elephant she gave you for your birthday.

If you really want to make a profit and draw a crowd, persuade your friends to have a multifamily sale with you, preferably at their house. Even at that, a good variety of junk will be hard to come by, and not everyone in your home will be cooperative. You must be prepared for the loss of a few arguments as you debate the pros and cons of selling your spouse's lucky underwear, his favorite grease-stained tee shirt, and his football bloopers video. But those will be nothing compared to the disagreements you will lose when you go through your children's belongings. It matters not that they haven't played with Mr. Potato Head in three years. The minute you stick a price tag on it, it becomes their favorite toy. Your only hope is to sneak such things out of the house while your children are sleeping.

Still, you're not done counting your losses yet. There is the loss of sleep, as you stay up all night agonizing whether your granny's denture cup is worth $1 or $1.25. There's the loss of privacy as garage sale regulars show up at your house before dawn, staked out on the road, ready to pounce at the first sign of life. There is your loss of dignity as you haggle with a stranger who wants you to take a quarter instead of fifty cents for your son's first pair of cowboy boots. Not only do they want to pay you pennies on the dollar for your most treasured memories, they want to buy anything not red hot or nailed down.

"Hey, lady, is this bike for sale?" they inquire.

"No, that is my son's. He just got it for his birthday," you insist.

"But it's in the garage. Are you sure it's not for sale? I'll give you ten bucks."

"No, it's not for sale."

"What about this baby stroller?" they say, circling like vultures.

"My baby is sleeping in that stroller!"

"I don't need a baby. I'll just take the stroller."

By far, though, the worst loss of all has to be the financial loss, as you realize you have spent more money buying your friend's junk than you have made selling your own. By forgetting your focus on selling instead of buying, you have lost all the profit for which you worked so hard. The whole thing turns out to be one big exercise in futility. Sure, you got through it, but you didn't make any profit. Instead, you have just got a head start on collecting more unwanted junk for the next garage sale, all because in the midst of the distractions you forgot the original purpose.

I am sad to admit it, but most of the time I run my life like I run my garage sales. I have a plan when the day starts, but by the time I get to the end, I've forgotten the real purpose. It's not that I am a total failure. I can keep my priorities in order just fine—for the first ten minutes of my day. That's when the rest of my household wakes up, ready to pounce on me at the first sign of life. I react in typical ADD fashion—Annoyed, Distracted, and Delirious. Between a husband, three children, and ten pets, a purpose as simple as brushing my teeth can get lost in the fury of the morning rush as I hurry between feeding cats and feeding kids, ironing shirts and ironing hair, finding socks and finding homework, giving out lunch money and giving out advice. In the blur, it might be two o'clock before I realize that I got sidetracked on my way to my toothbrush. What hope is there that as the hours wear on I will be able to regain any sense of purpose in my day?

Everything in life seems to be the tyranny of the urgent, even though I wake up each day with a renewed resolve that *today* will be the day the Lord has made. Today will be the day that I succeed at keeping my focus on the important, not the urgent. Before my feet hit the floor I tell God, "Good morning, Lord. It's Kim here and I am reporting for duty. Today is your day. I'm ready to get started." The first order of my day is, of course, to have some quiet time with the Lord.

So off I go in search of my Bible that I set down somewhere when someone asked me for something. Before I am able to locate it the assault begins. My daughter needs help with her pony tail, so promising myself I will get back to God, I start the search for the hairbrush, which I am looking for when the bell rings on the dryer, telling me that my son's basketball jersey is dry, which I plan to pack in his backpack until my husband asks me to find the checkbook so he can pay the overdue electric bill, which I am trying to locate when the dog throws up on the carpet, which I am attempting to clean up when I look at the clock and realize we are already late for school. Waiting at the red light in the car, I have the nagging feeling that I have forgotten something. What was it I was going to do first thing this morning? Oh, well, I console myself, it must not have been very important—and off I go to be tossed hither and yon by the winds of the rest of my day.

At the end of that day, when I fall into bed, hardly able to keep my eyes open, I chastise myself for all the potential that evaporated as I spent more on the junk then I ever intended. So, I promise myself that tomorrow really will be more profitable. Tomorrow I really am going to be more purposeful, more spiritual. Tomorrow I will work harder at making God's priorities my priorities. I won't get tangled in real life again. Clinging to the promise of Scarlet O'Hara, I drift off to sleep with the hope that "tomorrow is another day." Tomorrow, I'll ... *zzzzz*. I awake the next morning, refreshed by a blessed five hours of sleep, and eagerly report for duty.

"Here I am, Lord. Today really is your day. I'm ready to get started ... *ring, ring* ... right after I answer that phone."

Does any of this sound familiar? Have you had days when more got away from you than you had intended? Do you ever feel that you are spending too much time on the junk in life, losing more than you're gaining? Does the flood of people waiting to pounce on your time ever overwhelm you? Are others haggling for your priorities? If you answered yes to any or all of these questions, you are living a garage sale life—one that is more about loss than gain, more about panic than purpose. What you need to do is GET A LIFE— a *spiritual* life, that is.

I know what you're thinking. You would love to have a spiritual life, following God every day, but then who'd run your real life? Believe it or not, it is possible to live in the real world and find God's purpose for your life at the same time.

If it weren't, Jesus never would have prayed this prayer to His Father.

"My prayer is not that you take them out of the world but that you protect them from the evil one. They are not of the world, even as I am not of it. Sanctify them by the truth; your word is truth. As you sent me into the world, I have sent them into the world." (Jn 17:15-18, NIV).

It was God's idea to send us into the real world. According to Him we can live in that world and still find our spiritual purpose. We don't have to wait until all the distraction and interruptions are gone. God's purposes come in the midst of even the most unlikely moments.

"In him, according to the purpose of [God] who accomplishes all things according to the counsel of his will, we who first hoped in Christ have been destined and appointed to live for the praise of his glory" (Eph 1:11-12, RSV).

Do you see what I see? God works *all* things according to His purpose! God can work carpools and fender benders and illnesses and marriage and dinner parties and deadlines and business meetings and grocery shopping and vacations and grade cards and yard work and funerals and holidays and even garage sales *"according to the counsel of his will ... for the praise of his glory."*

We don't have to give up our real lives to get spiritual ones. Our real lives, no matter how crazy or mundane they seem, are spiritual because they are the ones God specifically appointed to us "according to the counsel of His will." Our lives aren't the distraction from a spiritual life. They *are* the spiritual life! And every detail, big and small, has one common purpose, "for the praise of His glory." The real challenge is keeping that purpose in focus in the midst of all the urgent moments of the day, even when others are waiting to pounce on our priorities, haggle over our time, and even tempt us to seek our glory instead of His.

Jesus faced these same kinds of demands and temptations. He knew that to stay focused on God's purpose for which each one of us has been called, we must continually put things in the right priority. He also knew that meant overcoming the biggest distraction of all—daily living.

> Therefore, I tell you, do not worry about your life, what you will eat or drink, or about your body, what you will wear. Is not life more important than food, and the body more important than clothes? Look at the birds of the air; they do not sow or reap or store away in barns, and yet your heavenly Father feeds them. And why do you worry about clothes? See how the lilies of the field grow. If that is how God clothes the grass of the field, which is here today and tomorrow is thrown into the fire, will he not much more clothe you, O you of little faith. So do not worry saying, "What shall we eat?" or "What shall we drink?" or "What shall we wear?" For the pagans run after all these things, and your heavenly Father knows that you need them. But seek first his kingdom and his righteousness, and all these things will be given to you as well. Therefore don't worry about tomorrow, for tomorrow will worry about itself.
>
> MATTHEW 6:25-34, NIV

Get a (Spiritual) Life

Whoa! Did Jesus ever peg me! I worry about what we will eat, if there is enough money, how I will cook dinner if I have to be at soccer practice, what we will wear if the laundry isn't done, if my clothes are fashionable enough, how I will ever fit into the size I used to, and a thousand other concerns of daily living. Too often my life can be described as "running after these things." Knowing what occupies my heart, Jesus gives me a reminder that He understands the pressures of my real life. We need to eat. We need clothes. We need to be in five places at once. Part of His purpose is to provide for us in all those ways. *B-u-t* (three little letters that can change everything) ... "life is more important" than these things. Jesus Himself, who knew what it was to have needs, gives us the secret to turning our ordinary lives into spiritual lives. "Seek *first* his kingdom and his righteousness, and [then] all these things will be given to you as well." It's all a matter of priorities. When seeking His kingdom is our first priority, trusting Him to provide all the other things as well, the most ordinary of our days brings praise to His glory—the most spiritual purpose we can have.

And what about tomorrow, with its long lists and paltry twenty-four hours? Well, Scarlet almost had it right. God works one day at a time and He tells us to do the same thing. "Therefore don't worry about tomorrow," not because tomorrow is another day, but because whatever tomorrow holds, God has a plan and a purpose that He is working, and He is already there ahead of us.

"And we know that in all things *God works for the good of those who love him, who have been called* according to

his purpose" (Rom 8:28, NIV, my emphasis).

There's that word again: *all*. God has a plan to use all the things in our lives as part of His purpose that will bring praise to *His* glory and good to us. Who will run your life if you make time to follow God even in the busy details of your day? God will, and He will work it for your good as well.

Are you ready to discover your real spiritual life? It's been there all along, just waiting to be given first place. To find it, you don't have to disown your family, quit your job, or move to a desert island. Your spiritual life can be found in the midst of your real life. All it requires is a desire to know God, put Him first, and follow Him wherever He leads you, each moment of the day. You will still make it to work on time, still be able to drive carpool, cook dinner, laugh with friends, take vacations, and even have a garage sale. The difference will be that as you look for why God has allowed the things in your day that He has, and you consider His priorities first, everything in your life will take on a spiritual dimension.

The part that may need some work is knowing what His priorities are so you can put them first and apply them to the moments of your day. If that is your goal, join me for the next thirty-one days as together we look for ways to make God's purposes our own. Begin by reading some moments from my real life. More often than not, these moments are real bizarre, real hectic, real crazy—but as real as the moments of *your* day. Through them, you will get to see the places in each of those days where God revealed opportunities for me to seek His kingdom first and find a spiritual purpose in my ordinary day.

After each story there is a short passage of God's Word to read and think about. These are what Jesus called the "words of truth" that would help our lives be set apart (sanctified) from the world around us. Use the journal page that follows each passage to record what you discover about God, His purposes, His priorities, and His promises. Make a plan for how you can "seek first His kingdom and righteousness" in the coming day and write it down. Talk with God about the pressures and demands you will face in the next twenty-four hours. Ask Him how He will "provide all other things as well" and what your part should be in that. Then trust that as you put first things first, He will see that all these things will work together for your good and to the praise of His glory. Finally, for your own encouragement, use the last space on your journal page to be specific about a purpose that God has shown you in the past twenty-four hours of your life.

As you not only read God's words but plan your day around His priorities, you will discover that you don't just have a life. You have a Spiritual Life!

Day 1
Starve a Fever

I didn't realize what a creature of habit I had become until time after time, my routine was submitted to the needs of someone else.

It started one Monday when my husband unexpectedly came home only one hour after leaving for work. With drooping eyes and flushed face he announced that he had been voted out of the office by a quorum of coworkers who all agreed his flu symptoms should be taken home. So there he stood, puny and sickly, in need of someone to give him care and compassion. Unfortunately, I was the only one home.

I did nudge him toward the bed and mumble something like, "I'm pretty busy this morning, but if you really need me just holler." I wanted to comfort and care for him, but Monday mornings were always busy. That was the year I coached elementary P.E. and I had to accomplish everything for the day in the three hours before I was due at school.

"Do you have time to make me soup?" Tony said in almost a whisper.

"Soup? Do you think you ought to eat? Aren't you supposed to starve a fever?"

But the helpless look in his flu-flushed eyes made it impossible to say no. As I served it on a tray and left the room I heard, "If it's not too much trouble, could I have a spoon to eat it with?"

Get a (Spiritual) Life

With a smile I complied, but made a mental note that he would be the first in line for the flu shot next year. When I got home from school with the kids later that afternoon, he was still in bed. I gave up any hope that still flickered of catching up on my list. I took stock and realized that all the things I hadn't gotten finished would have to roll over to Tuesday. I went to sleep holding on to the promise that "tomorrow is another day."

As it turned out, it was another day just like the last. Only this time my husband and my son were both home sick. Worse, though, they began to rally in the late afternoon and were constantly under foot. After I cleaned the kitchen, they came in and dirtied it up. When I needed to work on the computer, I found one of them at my desk. I got less done on Tuesday than I had on Monday. The good news was that they were finally better.

By Wednesday, they were back to their appointed places. Sadly, that's the one day of the week I am not home at all. With the little bit of time I did have that evening, my daughter, who is compassionate, wanted to bake a cake for a sick neighbor. (No, she is not adopted.) So, all the unfinished things remained until blessed Thursday, the one day I have no commitments, or so I thought.

Just as I returned that morning from taking the kids to school, sweet little Bailey called to say he had forgotten his homework—again. Of course, I drove it back to school and informed my son that he would be grounded from all media when he got home for his repeated forgetfulness. In hindsight, this was a mistake.

Get a (Spiritual) Life

As soon as Bailey got home he realized, almost with pride, "Mom, this is the first time I have ever been grounded. Since I have all this free time, why don't we play together?"

I don't know how it happened, probably it was all those cute freckles and his ability to see the silver lining in discipline, but the rest of the afternoon, when I should have been cleaning, writing, and making calls, I was playing a board game, jumping on the trampoline, and watching clouds with my grounded son.

It wasn't a very productive day for me. As a matter of fact, it wasn't even a productive week–that is to say, none of the things on my list got accomplished. Instead, it was profitable in ways I had not begun to imagine, all because I *inadvertently* fulfilled some key principles from God's word.

"You ... were called to be free. But, do not use your freedom to indulge the sinful nature; rather serve one another in love" (Gal 5:13). *"Though I am free and belong to no man, I make myself a slave to everyone, to win as many as possible [to the gospel]"* (1 Cor 9:19).

When we are willing to defer our rights in favor of another, we honor Christ by following His example and we glorify God through our loving service to those He loves. That is the kind of creature of habit I have been called to be.

My purpose today is to serve others by choice.

Psalm 64

O God, listen to my complaint. Do not let my enemies' threats overwhelm me. Protect me from the plots of the wicked, from the scheming of those who do evil. Sharp tongues are the swords they wield; bitter words are the arrows they aim. They shoot from ambush at the innocent, attacking suddenly and fearlessly. They encourage each other to do evil and plan how to set their traps. "Who will ever notice?" they ask. As they plot their crimes, they say, "We have devised the perfect plan!" Yes, the human heart and mind are cunning. But God himself will shoot them down. Suddenly, his arrows will pierce them. Their own words will be turned against them, destroying them. All who see it happening will shake their heads in scorn. Then everyone will stand in awe, proclaiming the mighty acts of God, realizing all the amazing things he does. The godly will rejoice in the Lord and find shelter in him. And those who do what is right will praise him.

Get a (Spiritual) Life

Seeking first things first ...

The Words of Truth reveal that God is ...
_____
_____
_____

The Words of Truth promise, warn, or teach me ...
_____
_____
_____

To seek "first His kingdom and righteousness" today I will ...
_____
_____
_____

The "other things" in my day that I must trust God for are ...
_____
_____
_____

One of God's purposes that He has shown me in my day is ...
_____
_____
_____
_____
_____
_____

Day 2
I Once Was Lost ...

If you find yourself in a local store and you hear over the intercom that a child is looking for his parent you can almost bet it's my middle son. Poor Bailey gets lost all too frequently.

As I arrive to retrieve my wayward child from the lost and found, I generally find him regaling the clerk with a story of the last time "we got lost" and he had to find us. Stores aren't the only places he gets lost. One particular Sunday, as often happens, our family took two separate cars to church. Tony left early and the kids and I followed later. Once there, we all scattered toward our classrooms. We didn't expect to see the kids again until after the worship service since they attend children's church.

After church, I was in a rush to get home. Since Hannah and Chase were easily found, I took them with me and asked Tony to bring Bailey. At home, a short time later, everyone was changed out of church clothes and gathered in the kitchen for lunch. About that time the phone rang. The voice on the other end asked, "May I speak to Bailey, please?"

As I turned to look around the room, Bailey was not in the kitchen.

I called for him. No answer. I looked at my husband. "Did he go upstairs when you got home?"

Panic registered on Tony's face. "I forgot him."

When I put the phone back to my ear, I could hear laughter

Get a (Spiritual) Life

on the other end. "It's OK. He's at the church with me," our friend revealed. "I just wondered if you knew he was missing."

We didn't. We made it a whole year without another major incident, but it was bound to happen. After four exhausting days at our family reunion, we were ready to come home. By the time we loaded everything in the motor home for the nine-hour trip back to Texas, all we wanted to do was sleep. While we were sympathetic to our chauffeurs, Tony in the motor home, and my dad caravanning behind us, we didn't let that stop the rest of us from napping until lunch.

Barely awake, we mechanically shuffled into a fast-food restaurant in rural Oklahoma, ate, and shuffled out again. As soon as we were in the motor home, everyone dived back into a pillow. With coffee in hand, Tony drove across the parking lot to the exit ramp. A few hundred feet later he prepared to enter traffic. He looked to the left and then to the right and then ...

"Is that Bailey running across the parking lot?" he asked matter-of-factly.

We all sat up in time to see Bailey, with a dripping ice cream cone in one hand, a napkin in the other, running after the motor home. We had no idea he could run so fast.

Later, when I asked him what he would have done if we had left him, he said, "I'd just get a job serving ice cream and earn money for the bus ride home." See, I didn't need to worry. Besides, we would have realized he was missing—about the time the news reported that police were looking for the parents of a child abandoned at a Braum's in Oklahoma.

So, there are two things to learn from this story. First, if you see a lost red-haired boy, he's probably ours. We'd appreciate a call. Second, searching for lost and precious things is important.

In Luke 15 Jesus tells three parables about searching for the lost. First there is a lost sheep, whose shepherd is willing to *"search until he finds it."* There is also the woman who loses one of her ten silver coins and diligently *"sweep(s) the house and search(es) carefully until she finds it."* And finally, there is the lost son whose father searched the road, waiting for his son's return, and then *"ran to his son, threw his arms around him and kissed him."*

No matter how someone finds himself lost, God reaches out to find him. *"For the Son of Man came to seek and to save what was lost"* (Lk 19:10)—and when what was lost is finally found, what a time of rejoicing that will be!

My purpose today is to seek and restore the lost ones in my life.

Psalm 40:1-5 (NIV)

I waited patiently for the Lord; he turned to me and heard my cry. He lifted me out of the slimy pit, out of the mud and mire; he set my feet on a rock and gave me a firm place to stand. He put a new song in my mouth, a hymn of praise to our God. Many will see and fear and put their trust in the Lord. Blessed is the man who makes the Lord his trust, who does not look to the proud, to those who turn aside to false gods. Many, O Lord my God, are the wonders you have done. The things you planned for us no one can recount to you; were I to speak and tell of them, they would be too many to declare.

Get a (Spiritual) Life

Seeking first things first ...

The Words of Truth reveal that God is ...
_____
_____
_____
_____

The Words of Truth promise, warn, or teach me ...
_____
_____
_____
_____

To seek "first His kingdom and righteousness" today I will ...
_____
_____
_____
_____

The "other things" in my day that I must trust God for are ...
_____
_____
_____
_____

One of God's purposes that He has shown me in my day is ...
_____
_____
_____

Day 3
The Fine Print

On a recent trip to California, I decided to book my flight through Priceline.com. It is a great way to buy inexpensive tickets, but you don't always get to choose your route. What you do get to choose are the departure and destination cities and the dates you want to fly. Then you offer a price and hope for the best.

Within five minutes I had a ticket for a phenomenal amount, but would also be arriving in California after my first meeting was scheduled.

I immediately called the airline that held my reservation. After I gave my sob story and requested to be moved to an earlier flight, I was told, "Oh sweetie, I'd love to change that for you, but that's a Priceline ticket. They're the only ones who can change it."

That seemed reasonable. I called the toll-free number she gave me and pleaded my case. Bob, from Priceline, was full of sympathy. "That is a terrible situation. Gosh, did you read our guidelines on the web site? I would love to help you, really I would, but as we state very plainly in our conditions, absolutely no changes can be made under any circumstances. Really, that is just too bad."

I actually thought Bob might cry. He was trained so well! I couldn't even complain. I had read the rules. Still, for the next week discontent settled in as I wrestled with my joy over saving money and my disappointment with the schedule. When

Get a (Spiritual) Life

I arrived at the airport on my travel day, I couldn't stop thinking about the nonstop flight that I knew would be leaving at the same time as mine, yet arriving hours earlier. As I waited almost an hour at the airline's ticket counter, stewing over my dilemma, I decided to try making the change one more time.

As I got closer to the front of the line I finally turned the situation over to God. "Lord, You know I want to go earlier, but You were so good to get me a ticket I could afford. If there is any way to change the flight, I am leaving it in Your hands. If not, I won't whine anymore."

As I stepped up to the counter and began to explain that I wanted to change flights, a humorless clerk named James stopped me before I even mentioned Priceline. "You cannot reroute a flight at this point," James insisted. "You must stay with your original flight plan. There can be no changes."

Obviously James did not train with Bob. "I understand," I said. "I was just hoping to change so that I wouldn't miss a meeting."

"I'm sorry. That is not possible," he said firmly as he began to closely examine his screen. Then with a puzzled look, he excused himself. "I'll be right back." He returned with a very cryptic look on his face. "It seems there is a storm approaching that may shut us down. We never do this, never, and it is only because of the storm, but I am giving you priority standby on the nonstop flight that arrives earlier." Then he added, "And I see this is a Priceline ticket. We never ever change those. I guess it is your lucky day."

All I could do was smile. "I wouldn't say I'm lucky," I told the clerk. "I'd say God graciously answered my prayers." James just stared, even more puzzled.

From there my bags were randomly chosen to be x-rayed and my tickets re-examined. As two clerks whispered over luggage stubs, I asked if there was a problem. "We show that you checked three bags and we see only two."

"That's right," I confirmed. "I checked only two."

"Well, we have three stubs. Are you traveling with someone invisible?"

How did they know? "As a matter of fact," I said with certainty, "I am."

With that, my invisible Companion and I were passed through security and given the very last seat on the nonstop flight.

Like Priceline, life is a place where we can't always choose our own route, but it is possible to choose our traveling companion. I don't know about you, but I choose to keep company with the One who promises that if I acknowledge Him in all my ways, He will direct my path (Prv 3:5-6).

"Now, to the King eternal, immortal, invisible, the only God, be honor and glory forever and ever. Amen" (1 Tm 1:17).

My purpose today is to walk with God, not run ahead.

Psalm 16

Keep me safe, O God, for I have come to you for refuge. I said to the Lord, "You are my Master! All the good things I have are from you." The godly people in the land are my true heroes! I take pleasure in them! Those who chase after other gods will be filled with sorrow. I will not take part in their sacrifices or even speak the names of their gods. Lord, you alone are my inheritance, my cup of blessing. You guard all that is mine. The land you have given me is a pleasant land. What a wonderful inheritance! I will bless the Lord who guides me; even at night my heart instructs me. I know the Lord is always with me. I will not be shaken, for he is right beside me. No wonder my heart is filled with joy, and my mouth shouts his praises! My body rests in safety. For you will not leave my soul among the dead or allow your godly one to rot in the grave. You will show me the way of life, granting me the joy of your presence and the pleasures of living with you forever.

Get a (Spiritual) Life

Seeking first things first ...

The Words of Truth reveal that God is ...

_____
_____
_____
_____

The Words of Truth promise, warn, or teach me ...

_____
_____
_____
_____

To seek "first His kingdom and righteousness" today I will ...

_____
_____
_____
_____

The "other things" in my day that I must trust God for are ...

_____
_____
_____
_____

One of God's purposes that He has shown me in my day is ...

_____
_____

Day 4
Murder, She Wrote

Over the past few years I have managed to kill off sundry superheroes, the Easter bunny, and the tooth fairy. The most recent casualty was Santa Claus, thus ending the last shred of hope my youngest child had in characters too good to be true.

I hadn't planned on shattering her faith so close to Christmas. I actually thought we would get at least one more year out of the old guy; after all, Hannah was only in third grade. She showed no signs of doubt that Santa could fly around the world delivering gifts to every boy and girl on the planet, with only one sleigh full of toys. Though her older brothers, Chase and Bailey, had known he was a fraud for some time, they continued to play along for their sister's sake. Hannah, then, had no reason to question flying reindeer, magic elves, or even why, occasionally, Santa's gifts came bearing price tags. That's why I was so unprepared when she announced that I was Santa.

One evening, I was explaining to her that I hadn't been able to locate the number one item on her Christmas list.

"Hannah, I don't want you to be disappointed, but I'm not sure I will find the baby lop-eared bunny you wanted this time of year. If you don't get it, remember that I tried," I told her.

"Well, if you can't, I'll just ask Santa," she replied matter-of-factly. Then tentatively she added, "Well, I guess you better look harder, because you are Santa."

It was really more of a question then a statement. At first, I just stared at her, until she said it again, and then again.

"You're Santa, Mom. I know you're really Santa."

Panicked, I had two choices. I could tell her an outright lie, or I could tell the truth. I chose something in between. With a wink, I pointed to her dad across the room.

Total horror registered on her face, followed closely by a look of crushing grief. Instantly, I knew my mistake. She didn't want to know the truth. Frantic to restore her hope, I pointed to myself as Santa, and then to the cat, as if the whole thing had been a joke, but it was too late. One giant crocodile tear rolled down her cheek.

"Daddy is Santa?" she said in disbelief. "But, last year I asked for a bunny and you said no, and Santa gave it to me anyway. He even left me a note. It was only Daddy? Why did you have to tell me?"

"Hannah, you said you knew it was me," I said desperately.

"I was only kidding," and the tears came faster. "Why did you ever tell me there was a Santa in the first place?"

"Look at the bright side," I said. "All those gifts really came from Mom and Dad, who love you so much more than Santa ever could. Doesn't that make you feel good?"

Her face reflected how lame she thought that was, so I made one last attempt to ease her disappointment. "Why don't we just enjoy the mystery of Santa and do the things we have always done. We can write our Santa letters, and leave cookies, and get up Christmas morning to Santa gifts. It can still be fun."

"Well," she said cynically, "let's not tell Chase and Bailey. At least they still believe."

How thankful I am that the greatest mystery of all is not a hoax, but a sure place for our hope. Through God's gift of Jesus Christ's birth, death, and resurrection we have the hope of eternal life that will never disappoint.

"It is impossible for God to lie, we who have fled to take hold of the hope offered to us may be greatly encouraged. We have this hope as an anchor for the soul, firm and secure. It enters the inner sanctuary behind the curtain, where Jesus, who went before us, has entered on our behalf" (Heb 6:18-20).

"[Since] we have a great Priest over the house of God, let us draw near to God with a sincere heart in full assurance of faith, having our hearts sprinkled to cleanse us from a guilty conscience and having our bodies washed with pure water. Let us hold unswervingly to the hope we profess, for He who promised is faithful" (Heb 10:21-23).

It may seem too good to be true, but hope in Christ is the only hope that will never disappoint.

> My purpose today is to know the God of Scripture, not the fairy tale I create.

Psalm 5

O Lord, hear me as I pray; pay attention to my groaning. Listen to my cry for help, my King and my God, for I will never pray to anyone but you. Listen to my voice in the morning, Lord. Each morning I bring my requests to you and wait expectantly. O God, you take no pleasure in wickedness; you cannot tolerate the slightest sin. Therefore, the proud will not be allowed to stand in your presence, for you hate all who do evil. You will destroy those who tell lies. The Lord detests murderers and deceivers. Because of your unfailing love, I can enter your house; with deepest awe I will worship at your Temple. Lead me in the right path, O Lord, or my enemies will conquer me. Tell me clearly what to do, and show me which way to turn. My enemies cannot speak one truthful word. Their deepest desire is to destroy others. Their talk is foul, like the stench from an open grave. Their speech is filled with flattery. O God, declare them guilty. Let them be caught in their own traps. Drive them away because of their many sins, for they rebel against you. But let all who take refuge in you rejoice; let them sing joyful praises forever. Protect them, so all who love your name may be filled with joy. For you bless the godly, O Lord, surrounding them with your shield of love.

Get a (Spiritual) Life

Seeking first things first ...

The Words of Truth reveal that God is ...

_____
_____
_____
_____

The Words of Truth promise, warn, or teach me ...

_____
_____
_____
_____

To seek "first His kingdom and righteousness" today I will ...

_____
_____
_____
_____

The "other things" in my day that I must trust God for are ...

_____
_____
_____
_____

One of God's purposes that He has shown me in my day is ...

_____
_____
_____

Day 5
All Thumbs

There are three places you won't find me—a seafood restaurant, a monster-truck pull, or a hobby store. The first two will never change, but for years I have been searching for a reason to visit a hobby store. I am a wanna-be hobbyist looking for a fun hobby.

My search began when I married a man with his own hobby, but golf didn't sound very leisurely to me. Instead of joining him, I took up sewing. My first project was a Simplicity skirt, but as I unfolded the pattern, I knew there would be nothing simple about learning to sew. Fortunately, I had a friend who explained the basics, then left me with a piece of advice: "Pay attention to details."

My new fun hobby was turning into a lot of work. Details are painfully tedious and not the least bit fun, yet I stayed with it to the end. Imagine my surprise when my skirt was a success. The hem was straight, the size was right, and I liked the pockets backward.

Euphoric about my triumph, I decided to make something to wear to my husband's college graduation, only three days away. Every spare moment of those seventy-two hours was devoted to cutting and pinning. The night before his graduation I worked until dawn, but still found that I had to cut corners. I left seams unfinished and hems only basted until, at last, the final button was whipped into place.

Running late, I proudly donned my new homemade outfit

and drove to the graduation. Though I had gotten no sleep, there was a spring in my step as I paraded my new frock across the crowded parking lot. My head was held high as the periwinkle taffeta swirled around my knees. It was so high, I almost didn't notice my skirt dropping around my ankles, leaving me standing in the parking lot in my slip. As onlookers stared, I scooped the taffeta back around my waist in humiliation. Apparently, in my haste, I had forgotten to secure that last button with a knot. Details, details, details.

Next, I tried gourmet cooking, but it was not a good fit. It turned out to be yet another hobby where details were important. My husband will never let me forget Hamburger Bisquick Pie. Today, a gourmet meal at our house is anything not served in a plastic container.

Clearly, I needed to experiment outside the domestic realm. Ceramics seemed a good place to start. I made picture frames, ashtrays, lamps, and ceramic geese. Though I did enjoy it, on average I broke one piece of green ware for every one I completed. I needed something less fragile, so I enrolled in a watercolor class. I have long felt that I have the soul of an artist. Sadly, I didn't get the talent of one.

Having no luck with creative hobbies, I decided to try athletics. The first was softball. Though I'd never played a sport before, I knew I could learn. What could be simpler than hitting a ball with a bat? (Brain surgery, perhaps?) On the rare occasions I did make contact, I got a cramp in my leg as I sprinted to first base. My spirit was willing, but, alas, my body was weak.

Since then I've tried volleyball, biking, gardening, cross-stitching, running, singing, and basketball. I'll spare you the details but clearly I have no aptitude for any of these. Still, I'm not giving up. Somewhere, there is a hobby just perfect for an energetic, uncoordinated, tone deaf, out-of-shape-but-willing enthusiast. I plan to keep searching until I find the one meant just for me.

In a sense, spiritual gifts are a lot like hobbies. They, too, are not one-size-fits-all. Instead, they are spiritual abilities handpicked by God and given individually to those in the body of Christ. Just like hobbies, there are a variety of gifts. There are gifts of teaching, administration, serving, encouraging, giving, and showing mercy, or one of many others described in Scripture. While finding a hobby is questionable, having a spiritual gift is a certainty.

"To each one the manifestation of the Spirit is given for the common good.... He gives them to each one, just as he determines" (1 Cor 12:7-11, NIV).

Whatever our gift, God's desire is that we search for it and use it.

"Don't neglect your gift" (1 Tm 4:14). *"Each one should use whatever gift he has received to serve others"* (1 Pt 4:10).

Spiritual gifts are for all spiritual wanna-be's, and you don't even have to be coordinated.

My purpose today is to use my spiritual gift for the common good.

Psalm 26

Declare me innocent, O Lord, for I have acted with integrity; I have trusted in the Lord without wavering. Put me on trial, Lord, and cross-examine me. Test my motives and affections. For I am constantly aware of your unfailing love, and I have lived according to your truth. I do not spend time with liars or go along with hypocrites. I hate the gatherings of those who do evil, and I refuse to join in with the wicked. I wash my hands to declare my innocence. I come to your altar, O Lord, singing a song of thanksgiving and telling of all your miracles. I love your sanctuary, Lord, the place where your glory shines. Don't let me suffer the fate of sinners. Don't condemn me along with murderers. Their hands are dirty with wicked schemes, and they constantly take bribes. But I am not like that; I do what is right. So in your mercy, save me. I have taken a stand, and I will publicly praise the Lord.

Get a (Spiritual) Life

Seeking first things first ...

The Words of Truth reveal that God is ...

_____
_____
_____
_____

The Words of Truth promise, warn, or teach me ...

_____
_____
_____
_____

To seek "first His kingdom and righteousness" today I will ...

_____
_____
_____
_____

The "other things" in my day that I must trust God for are ...

_____
_____
_____
_____

One of God's purposes that He has shown me in my day is ...

_____
_____
_____

Day 6
Dallas Dolls

What a girl day I had! From start to finish it was one of those joyous days any man would hate. It started with a car ride to Dallas with four other women to attend a Bible study conference. We decided we would drive up early and spend the afternoon preparing ourselves spiritually—at the mall.

Actually, for the four women riding with me, their spiritual preparation started when they got in my car. Entrusting their lives into my inattentive driving hands was itself an act of faith. For one of them who knows me well, I'm sure she felt like Queen Esther of old, facing her dangerous duty proclaiming, "If I perish, I perish." I was so moved by her steadfast courage, I actually tried to focus on the road.

That may sound easy, but when five women get together in a car, driving gets little attention. After all, there are entertaining tales to be told, snacks to be passed, and accessories to be admired. It's no wonder more women have accidents. What do men do when they drive but try to pass the guy in the next lane? They won't stop for a bathroom break because the cars they already passed will get ahead again. We were too busy laughing to compete for the lead.

When we finally made it to the city (with just one pit stop, thank you) we drove straight to an upscale North Dallas mall. After a very girlish lunch of chicken salad it was time to shop. Two of our friends had pressing needs and went off

Get a (Spiritual) Life

together in search of chic handbags, so we agreed to meet them three hours later. In the meantime, we realized that of the three of us remaining, all we needed was a gift card. What were we going to do to fill the next three hours?

Well, it was a girl weekend, so we did the girly-est thing we could think of doing. We went to the Neiman-Marcus day spa for a manicure. It was my first manicure and my first trip to Neiman's and it was glorious! We took turns in the manicurist's chair, being offered refreshments and pampered like we were royalty. I wouldn't be surprised to find a Neiman-Marcus manicurist in heaven with that wonderful little bottle of oil she so expertly massaged into our hands and arms. It was heavenly. Hoping it would be this new friend, I took just a minute to share Jesus with the lovely Korean manicurist. I hope I'll see her there.

Neiman's was also hosting a renowned hair stylist from New York City that day who offered free hair consultations— by appointment only, of course. I was able to get one of those coveted appointments. Waiting in a chair at the end of a long row of others, with a friend offering encouragement, I was given my own salon attendant. As we waited, I was offered everything from an $85 hairbrush (gulp) to a $250 sample pack of necessary hair products.

Finally, the maestro approached and commanded me to stand. When I started to speak, he abruptly put his finger to his lips. "No, No," he instructed with a heavy French accent. "You mustn't speak. You must listen to what I say and you must do it *right away*. First, you have a very beautiful face." (I wonder how long he practiced to say that with a straight face to two hundred women.) Then he added, "But you are doing nothing to help it." (I think I was being insulted.) "Right away you must cut your hair. And your color is very yesterday. You must catch up with the rest of us and you must do it immediately." He proceeded to tell me exactly how to cut and color my hair and which products I needed to use immediately to save myself from spontaneously combusting.

I left the salon, laughing with my friend at the stylist's concern for my scandalous hair. The rest of the conference weekend was just as joyful and just as girlish, with late-night talking, hanging out in the coffee shop, and enjoying friends.

With so many trials and duties that we must endure day to day, it is a wonderful reminder that God has also given us many things to enjoy.

"Put (your) hope in God, who richly provided us with everything for our enjoyment" (1 Tm 6:17, emphasis added).

The Christian life is a joyous one, so remember, *"a joyful heart is good medicine."* Go ahead, laugh out loud, go bowling with a friend, or get a manicure. Enjoy the abundant life that God has given you, *"and you must do it right away."*

My purpose today is to laugh and enjoy the life God has given me.

Psalm 34

I will praise the Lord at all times. I will constantly speak his praises. I will boast only in the Lord; let all who are discouraged take heart. Come, let us tell of the Lord's greatness; let us exalt his name together. I prayed to the Lord, and he answered me, freeing me from all my fears. Those who look to him for help will be radiant with joy; no shadow of shame will darken their faces. I cried out to the Lord in my suffering, and he heard me. He set me free from all my fears. For the angel of the Lord guards all who fear him, and he rescues them. Taste and see that the Lord is good. Oh, the joys of those who trust in him! Let the Lord's people show him reverence, for those who honor him will have all they need. Even strong young lions sometimes go hungry, but those who trust in the Lord will never lack any good thing.

Get a (Spiritual) Life

Seeking first things first ...

The Words of Truth reveal that God is ...

_____
_____
_____
_____

The Words of Truth promise, warn, or teach me ...

_____
_____
_____
_____

To seek "first His kingdom and righteousness" today I will ...

_____
_____
_____
_____

The "other things" in my day that I must trust God for are ...

_____
_____
_____
_____

One of God's purposes that He has shown me in my day is ...

_____
_____
_____

Day 7
Birds of a Feather

When it comes to submission, there are a few places I still struggle. One is when my husband insists he knows the best hairstyles for our sons. He'd be right if they were in the Marines, but since they're not, I have been slightly defiant by letting them grow hair beyond the stubble stage. More recently, though, I've had to struggle with his decision that we would not be adding any more pets to our family's menagerie. When our fourteen-year-old son mentioned that he would like a ferret for his birthday, my husband looked incredulous.

"We've got too many mangy animals around here as it is," he declared.

Too many? Probably, but mangy? Both dogs may be smelly but they're disease-free. The three cats keep one another impeccably groomed and I don't think snakes can be mangy. That leaves only five snails, one slightly balding rabbit, and one parakeet who is definitely mean, but not mangy.

Still, Tony laid down the law. "We're not getting any more animals."

"You heard your dad," I concurred obediently. "No more pets."

Submission wasn't so hard—for one day. Then the phone rang.

"Bailey said that he wanted to buy Connor's gerbil," my neighbor said. "Does he still want it?"

My son was overjoyed at the news that this nifty little gerbil was on the market, and for only five dollars. "Come on, Mom! Let's go get my gerbil," he said with allowance in hand.

It wasn't until we pulled into my friend's driveway that I remembered my husband's mandate. I knew that Tony probably wouldn't even notice such a small addition; still I was trying to work on that submission thing.

"Bailey, let me just call Daddy real quick and make sure this is OK with him." Pulling him from a lunch meeting, I caught Tony on his cell phone. "Honey, I'm just checking. When you said 'no more pets' you didn't mean the gerbil Bailey already told Connor he would buy from him, did you?"

"Oh, no, of *course* I didn't mean the gerbil," he said with a bit of sarcasm.

"Great. Thanks honey." I was glad I cleared that up. "Daddy says, go for it."

The only problem with getting one new pet is that we have three children. As soon as we brought it home, everyone wanted one just like it. Hannah already has a cat, a dog, and a rabbit that I take care of, so it was easy to say no to her. Chase was a harder case.

"Mom, come on. Take me up to the pet store so I can get a gerbil. I will use my birthday money and it can live in the cage with Bailey's. Please, Mom."

Of course I said no the obligatory twelve times, then we all got in the car. At the pet store, gerbils were quickly forgotten.

"Hey, Mom, they have a chinchilla. I'll buy it and you can buy the cage."

I didn't need any help saying no to that proposition. I had plenty of litter pans to clean already. As I tried to get him back on task with the gerbil, his younger brother introduced him to the flock of cockatiels by the front door. When that yellow and gray bird perched itself imperiously on Chase's shoulder, it was love at first peck.

"Please, Mom, I have enough birthday money."

"That's not a gerbil and Dad said we couldn't have any more pets." Then I had a thought. "Bailey did say he wanted to set that mean parakeet free. If he did, and you bought this one, we wouldn't actually be getting any more pets. We'd still have the same number." That made sense to everyone. So, Chase bought the bird, the parakeet was freed, and because we don't have any more pets than we did before, we stayed within the letter of the law. I call that creative submission.

In the spiritual sense, that same kind of wrangling often keeps me within the letter of God's laws, yet far from complete submission. Outwardly I comply, but inwardly my heart has not yielded at all.

"For the mind-set of the flesh is hostile to God because it does not submit itself to God's law.... You, however, are not in the flesh, but in the Spirit, since the Spirit of God lives in you" (Rom 8:7-9). *"But now we have been released from the law ... so that we may serve in the new way of the Spirit and not in the old letter of the law"* (Rom 7:6).

If you have been practicing creative submission with God, wrangling and maneuvering within the law, try a new way that starts from the heart.

My purpose today is to submit with a whole heart to God's authority.

Psalm 1

Oh, the joys of those who do not follow the advice of the wicked, or stand around with sinners, or join in with scoffers. But they delight in doing everything the Lord wants; day and night they think about his law. They are like trees planted along the riverbank, bearing fruit each season without fail. Their leaves never wither, and in all they do, they prosper. But this is not true of the wicked. They are like worthless chaff, scattered by the wind. They will be condemned at the time of judgment. Sinners will have no place among the godly. For the Lord watches over the path of the godly, but the path of the wicked leads to destruction.

Get a (Spiritual) Life

Seeking first things first ...

The Words of Truth reveal that God is ...

_____
_____
_____
_____
_____

The Words of Truth promise, warn, or teach me ...

_____
_____
_____
_____

To seek "first His kingdom and righteousness" today I will ...

_____
_____
_____
_____

The "other things" in my day that I must trust God for are ...

_____
_____
_____
_____

One of God's purposes that He has shown me in my day is ...

_____
_____

Day 8
Weenies Rule

Nowhere in the fine print did the ski brochure say anything about emergency medical assistance. Nor did it warn of the dangers of two-hundred-foot drops, strategically placed trees, or rude Scotsmen. Had these details been disclosed I might not have taken the trip.

I am a novice skier. In fact, I have the honor of being part of a foursome of women dubbed "The Green Weenies." While others in our contingent conquer the blue and black expert trails, we proudly warm up on the bunny slopes.

After four years, I guess I could be better, but after all, that amounts to only twelve actual ski days. So, I prefer to focus on the amazing progress I have made in less than two weeks. In fact, this year, my comrades and I actually improved and were encouraged to try the blue slopes by our more experienced friends, whom we lovingly call "The Hot Mamas," partly because they are so hot on the slopes, and partly because some are hitting menopause. But like true weenies, we declined, happy to be green forever.

It was with this resolve that I boarded a lift on the last day of our ski trip. My companions were in the chairs ahead of me, and I was seated with a stranger for the ride up the mountain. The long ascent to the top gave us time to get acquainted.

I started the conversation by admiring his unique, exceptionally long skis. "I've never seen skis like that. You must be a pretty serious skier," I complimented.

In a decidedly foreign accent he admitted the obvious.

Get a (Spiritual) Life

"Sure, I've been skiing most of my life."

Clearly we would not be swapping ski stories, so I changed the subject. "Where are you from?"

"I come from Scotland. That's my fiancé and my son behind us. We are getting married on the slopes on Tuesday," he said with some pride. "But we are a wee worried that the weather might be bad."

Every bride's nightmare is that her goggles will fog up before she can say "I do." I sympathized and in the spirit of nation building I offered my congratulations and promised to pray for cooperative weather. Eventually our ride came to a close and we prepared to unload. I adjusted my poles, scooted to the edge of the chair, focused on keeping my skis uncrossed, and prepared to launch myself to the ground. He simply stood up. Unfortunately, he stood on my left ski.

"Oops, excuse me. I think we ..." and down I went, landing hard on my tailbone. The Scotsman never looked back, a clear case of hit and run. I, on the other hand, wasn't moving at all.

When I failed to get up, I drew a crowd. "Are you OK?" "Can you move your legs?" "Do you know where you are?" (Were they talking to me?)

Soon the ski patrol was asking the same questions. Within minutes I was bundled into an emergency basket with an oxygen mask strapped on. Dizzy and nauseous, I still managed to catch sight of my friends behind the paramedics—aiming their camera at me!

That was the picture that should have been on the front of the ski brochure.

Under it the caption could read, "Excitement, Thrills, and *Suffering* Guaranteed." The blue skis and snow capped mountains told only half the story. That was the half I signed up for.

I bought into the Christian life like I did the ski trip, without looking closely at that heavenly brochure. All I saw were peaceful rolling hills, sheep in the field, and a mighty Shepherd standing watch. My caption read, "Come to Paradise, where the grass is always green and you'll dwell in safety forever."

It is on the other side, the one most of us never turn over, where the details are found. That side would show a picture of the same mighty Shepherd, nailed to a cross on the only path leading to those rolling green hills. Its caption tells the rest of the story: "Free Ticket to Paradise for anyone willing to come this way."

"If anyone would come after me, he must deny himself and take up his cross and follow me. For whoever wants to save his life will lose it, but whoever loses his life for me will find it" (Mt 16:24-25).

"If you suffer as a Christian, do not be ashamed, but praise God that you bear that name.... To this you were called, because Christ suffered for you, leaving you an example, that you should follow in His steps.... And when the Chief Shepherd appears, you will receive the crown of glory that will never fade away" (1 Pt 4:16; 2:21; 5:4, NIV).

Planning a trip to real Paradise? Excitement, thrills, and suffering are guaranteed along the way, but your ticket has been paid in full and the final destination is out of this world.

My purpose today is to endure suffering with Paradise on my mind.

Psalm 21

I look up to the mountains—does my help come from there? My help comes from the Lord, who made the heavens and the earth! He will not let you stumble and fall; the one who watches over you will not sleep. Indeed, he who watches over Israel never tires and never sleeps. The Lord himself watches over you! The Lord stands beside you as your protective shade. The sun will not hurt you by day, nor the moon at night. The Lord keeps you from all evil and preserves your life. The Lord keeps watch over you as you come and go, both now and forever.

Get a (Spiritual) Life

Seeking first things first ...

The Words of Truth reveal that God is ...
_____
_____
_____
_____

The Words of Truth promise, warn, or teach me ...
_____
_____
_____
_____

To seek "first His kingdom and righteousness" today I will ...
_____
_____
_____
_____

The "other things" in my day that I must trust God for are ...
_____
_____
_____

One of God's purposes that He has shown me in my day is ...
_____
_____
_____

Day 9
IOU and UO Him

Ever looked closely at a $20 bill? You would see the United States of America banner waving across the top, President Jackson looking wistfully at us through time, and bold numbers indicating its value. On the flip side are the White House and the motto we know by heart, "In God We Trust." However, it is the little notation on the front that reads, "This is legal tender for all debts, public and private," that is most meaningful to me.

That about covers my finances. I have public debts and I have private debts. What I keep running out of is the legal tender. Invariably, the pizza guy arrives and I'm out of cash. I need bread, but I have no dough. Everyone needs lunch money, but all I can dig from the bottom of my purse is thirty-two cents and a furry mint. So what's a cashless mom supposed to do? I borrow from my kids, of course.

Not because I have to, mind you. It's all part of my greater plan to teach them financial concepts. Here's how it works. Once a month their dad hands out allowance. They set aside 10 percent for savings and 10 percent for giving. The rest is to spend—or for me to borrow.

If I need to run to the store I take a poll. "Who's got $5?" This is where the training in financial wisdom begins. The child I used to borrow from the most caught on the quickest. Now, he can never seem to find his wallet when I need money. He's apparently learned *"The prudent man sees danger and hides [his wallet] ..."* (Prv 27:12).

My middle son has also learned prudence. He counters my request for a loan with, "Sure, Mom, you can borrow $5. Would you just write me a check for it?"

Only my youngest still gives me unfettered access to her life's savings. She offers eagerly, without a word about IOU's or repayment schedules.

She knows what it is to follow Jesus' teaching.

"Give to everyone who asks of you, and whoever takes away what is yours, do not demand it back ... and lend, expecting nothing in return; and your reward will be great ..." (Lk 6:30, 35).

I could see each of their philosophies at work when our family set out to fill a special bank for war refugees. Our goal was to fill it with silver coins. We searched couch cushions, car ashtrays, piggy banks, purses, dresser tops, and pockets, gathering more than $20 in loose change. Everyone was very generous.

Then we reminded the kids to also bring their personal giving envelopes to church. Change is one thing, but greenbacks are another. After calculating 10 percent of each allowance, our oldest son questioned, again, why his 10 percent was twice as much as that of his younger siblings. "Because your allowance is twice as much," we reminded him.

His younger brother's more practical approach was to verify the facts. "Who gets this money and exactly how much do I have to give?" With that clarification he counted out, to the penny and no more, his 10 percent.

Get a (Spiritual) Life

Our youngest had questions, too. With her $1 in hand, she asked, "Do you think 10 percent is enough? Maybe I should give more." Knowing her limited funds I was tempted to tell her it was plenty. Instead I sent her to a wiser financial advisor. "Sweetie, why don't you go and pray about it? Ask God, then do what you think He is telling you."

The next time I saw her we were leaving for church. I looked down and she had $1 in her hand—plus her entire month's allowance. "God wants me to give it to a missionary to tell about Jesus," she said with bright joyful eyes.

"Whoever sows sparingly will also reap sparingly, and whoever sows generously will also reap generously. Each man should give what he has decided in his heart to give, not reluctantly or under compulsion, for God loves a cheerful giver.... You will be made rich in every way so that you can be generous on every occasion ... [resulting] in thanksgiving to God" (2 Cor 9:6-7, 11, NIV).

My daughter was rich in joy because she took the occasion to sow generously into the kingdom of God. That's something we cannot do when we hide it away, give out of obligation, or expect something in return. She learned that while I may be a bad debt risk, God is not.

Legal tender can't buy treasure in heaven, and it can't pay the debt Christ already paid for us, but it can be used for God's glory now, when "In God We Trust" is the motto of our heart and God Himself is our financial advisor.

My purpose today is to give generously.

Psalm 24

The earth is the Lord's, and everything in it. The world and all its people belong to him. For he laid the earth's foundation on the seas and built it on the ocean depths. Who may climb the mountain of the Lord? Who may stand in his holy place? Only those whose hands and hearts are pure, who do not worship idols and never tell lies. They will receive the Lord's blessing and have right standing with God their savior. They alone may enter God's presence and worship the God of Israel. Open up, ancient gates! Open up, ancient doors, and let the King of glory enter. Who is the King of glory? The Lord, strong and mighty, the Lord, invincible in battle. Open up, ancient gates! Open up, ancient doors, and let the King of glory enter. Who is the King of glory? The Lord Almighty—he is the King of glory.

Get a (Spiritual) Life

Seeking first things first ...

The Words of Truth reveal that God is ...
_____
_____
_____
_____

The Words of Truth promise, warn, or teach me ...
_____
_____
_____
_____

To seek "first His kingdom and righteousness" today I will ...
_____
_____
_____
_____

The "other things" in my day that I must trust God for are ...
_____
_____
_____

One of God's purposes that He has shown me in my day is ...
_____
_____
_____

Day 10
This Little Piggy Stayed Home

A while back I developed a severe foot pain that made me whimper with every step, yet I resisted seeing a physician. Only weaklings run to the doctor with every twinge. The proud wait until they're almost lame.

Eventually, my family forced me to call the podiatrist. For the first time, I noticed the shabby condition of my feet. I tried to disguise the neglect by painting my toenails Fabulous Fuchsia and washing them with antibacterial soap. I even applied lavender lotion, but you know what they say about a silk purse and a sow's ear.

I shouldn't have bothered. The doctor took no notice. Instead, he focused on my foot as if he were a gypsy fortune-teller, able to read the future in corns and bunions. What he predicted was that I would soon need a "minor procedure" to surgically remove a pinched nerve.

The cure sounded worse than the cause. "Isn't there some pill I could take or maybe a corrective shoe?"

I left his office determined that time alone would heal my foot. It will get better. It will get better. It will get better. It didn't get better. Six agonizing months later, I called the office, begging for surgery. Suddenly, I was in a hurry. "I don't want to see the doctor again. Just give me the earliest day for the procedure."

"Be at the surgery center tomorrow at 6:30," the nurse instructed, "and don't eat or drink past midnight."

Get a (Spiritual) Life

After clarifying that this was 6:30 A.M. she was talking about, I reluctantly agreed, but being there before sun-up would require caffeine. I was sure her instructions didn't exclude coffee. I dressed with loose pant legs that could be pulled out of the doctor's way, and assured my husband I did not need a ride.

"It's just a minor procedure. Go to work. I'll call you when I get home." Against his better judgment, he let me go.

When I arrived at the surgery center I met the receptionist, who kept looking toward the door as if she were expecting someone. Finally she asked, "Are you here alone? Who drove you?"

"I did. I'm just having a minor procedure," I told her as I settled in to fill out pages of forms. Then I met with Nurse Linda, whose first question was, predictably, "Who is going to drive you home?"

I was beginning to see a pattern. "I'll be driving myself."

"Hon, you can't drive after being sedated."

Sedated? Didn't she read my chart? "This is a minor procedure!" I insisted, even as they were handing me a hospital gown and hooking up the IV. "I suppose you won't let me keep my cell phone, so if my kids call, tell them Mommy's been drugged and they'll have to call back."

Their response to my levity was to wheel me into an icy cold room and strap me to a table. Boy, was I glad I had had coffee. As I dozed off, I could only hope that they were taking my minor procedure more seriously than I had.

Now that I'm all healed, I have to admit that putting myself in the doctor's hands was long overdue. It seems I suffered needlessly for far too long.

How often that is true of our inner wounds as well. Broken-hearted, despairing, and hopeless, we hold emotional hurts inside, willing ourselves to be brave, to endure, to pull ourselves up by the bootstraps. We are in good company because we are not the first to suffer alone. King David knew what it was to endure a crushed spirit.

"I am weary with my sighing; every night I make my bed swim, I dissolve my couch with my tears. My eye has wasted away with grief ..." (Ps 6:6-7).

But he also knew the only One to turn to when the wound cut to his very soul.

"Be gracious to me, O Lord, for I am pining away; Heal me, O Lord, ... for my soul is greatly dismayed.... Return, Lord and rescue my soul ..." (Ps 6:2-3, NIV).

And God did not, and will not, disappoint because *"A bruised reed he will not break, and a smoldering wick he will not snuff out"* (Mt 12:20, NIV). The Great Physician takes our wounds seriously and is Himself the balm of healing.

God doesn't want us to be brave and endure our suffering alone. He invites all who are weak and helpless to run to the only Physician who can *"[heal] the brokenhearted and [bind] up their wounds"* (Ps 147:3, NIV).

My purpose today is to share my hurts with
God and receive His comfort.

Psalm 6

O Lord, do not rebuke me in your anger or discipline me in your rage. Have compassion on me, Lord, for I am weak. Heal me, Lord, for my body is in agony. I am sick at heart. How long, O Lord, until you restore me? Return, O Lord, and rescue me. Save me because of your unfailing love. For in death, who remembers you? Who can praise you from the grave? I am worn out from sobbing. Every night tears drench my bed; my pillow is wet from weeping. My vision is blurred by grief; my eyes are worn out because of all my enemies. Go away, all you who do evil, for the Lord has heard my crying. The Lord has heard my plea; the Lord will answer my prayer. May all my enemies be disgraced and terrified. May they suddenly turn back in shame.

Get a (Spiritual) Life

Seeking first things first ...

The Words of Truth reveal that God is ...
_____
_____
_____
_____

The Words of Truth promise, warn, or teach me ...
_____
_____
_____
_____

To seek "first His kingdom and righteousness" today I will ...
_____
_____
_____

The "other things" in my day that I must trust God for are ...
_____
_____
_____
_____

One of God's purposes that He has shown me in my day is ...
_____
_____
_____
_____

Day 11
To Have and to Hold

It's finally here—that day I have dreaded since the doctor announced, "It's a boy."

I will never forget the first moments alone with my son. In the middle of the night, while the rest of the world slept, I cuddled my precious baby boy and made him the promise mommies have been making their sons for thousands of generations.

"I promise, from this day forward, to love you and care for you and at all costs to protect you. No matter what, I will always be your best girl."

That promise was reciprocated, as it has been by sons to their mothers for thousands of generations, when at five years old, little Chase announced, "Mom, when I grow up, I'm going to marry you."

Though I reminded him that I was already married to his father, he was unconcerned. "That's OK," he said, "I'll marry Daddy, too."

Yet as he wrapped his chubby little arms around my neck, sealing his promise with a kiss, I knew one day he'd discover the other girls in the world. "One day," a little voice said, "he's going to forget that promise."

It's finally happened. The day came when my fourteen-year-old, five-foot-ten, 145-pound, blue-eyed, football-playing son asked if he could invite a girl to the homecoming game.

But, I wanted to say, *I'm* you're best girl, remember?

Get a (Spiritual) Life

Instead, I panicked and said, "Absolutely not!"—at which time Chase turned to my husband, as he has learned to do whenever I'm unreasonable, and said, "Talk to her, would you, Dad?"

At first I was not disposed to take my husband's counsel seriously. After all, look what happened after *he* started dating girls—he got married! It just wasn't worth the risk. It didn't matter to me that the girl Chase wanted to invite was a kindhearted, respectful, precious Christian girl. She was a girl.

Still, I did want to give at least the appearance of fairness. I would never want to be accused of being closed-minded. So I inquired of some trusted buddies who had already been down this road with their sons. These now former friends all gave the same advice, "It's time."

Time for what, I ask you? Time for him to abandon his family? Time for him to take his focus off the important things like school and sports? Time to forget his promise?

Yes, I suppose it was time.

Well, if that's the case then the next question was: How do we prepare Chase for the challenges of female companionship? Is he ready for lessons like, every woman is entitled to change her mind as many times as she sees fit? What about the universal truth that women generally run in a different time zone than male counterparts? It's not Pacific, Central, or Eastern Standard Time. Women operate in NST—"No Standard Time." Should we tell him that girls, being little women but with less emotional control, will try to interpret his feelings through every twitch of his eye, every hesitation in his voice, and every forgotten phone call?

No, these are truths no man understands. Let's stick to things like opening the door, rising when a young lady approaches, and how pitching arms are ruined forever by handholding. The rest of the lessons he will learn in time. Until then, he has already left his first broken heart behind, along with a promise he could never keep. But then, as a mom, I never expected that he would. I am just thankful that, for a while, I was his best girl.

Promises are often like the ones Chase and I made. They are made with all sincerity, but are sometimes impossible to keep. It's hard to understand, then, a God who always keeps His promises—even the most unbelievable—like when God promised, *"Never will I leave you; never will I forsake you"* (Heb 13:5).

Never? Will there never be a time when God will change His mind? What if I fail Him? What if He forgets? What if He is not able? Will I really always be God's greatest love?

"'Though the mountains be shaken and the hills be removed, yet my unfailing love for you will not be shaken nor my covenant of peace be removed,' says the Lord, who has compassion on you" (Is 54:10).

A time will never come when His promise, sealed not with a kiss but with the blood of Christ, will ever be broken.

My purpose today is to trust God's promises and share them with others.

Psalm 144

Bless the Lord, who is my rock. He gives me strength for war and skill for battle. He is my loving ally and my fortress, my tower of safety, my deliverer. He stands before me as a shield, and I take refuge in him. He subdues the nations under me. O Lord, what are mortals that you should notice us, mere humans that you should care for us? For we are like a breath of air; our days are like a passing shadow. Bend down the heavens, Lord, and come down. Touch the mountains so they billow smoke. Release your lightning bolts and scatter your enemies! ... I will sing a new song to you, O God! I will sing your praises with a ten-stringed harp. For you grant victory to kings! You are the one who rescued your servant David. Save me from the fatal sword! Rescue me from the power of my enemies.... May our sons flourish in their youth like well-nurtured plants. May our daughters be like graceful pillars, carved to beautify a palace. May our farms be filled with crops of every kind. May the flocks in our fields multiply by the thousands, even tens of thousands, and may our oxen be loaded down with produce. May there be no breached walls, no forced exile, no cries of distress in our squares. Yes, happy are those who have it like this! Happy indeed are those whose God is the Lord.

Get a (Spiritual) Life

Seeking first things first ...

The Words of Truth reveal that God is ...

___

The Words of Truth promise, warn, or teach me ...

___

To seek "first His kingdom and righteousness" today I will ...

___

The "other things" in my day that I must trust God for are ...

___

One of God's purposes that He has shown me in my day is ...

___

Day 12
Lost and Found

It's not easy to lose an almost full-grown child, but after an extensive search, my teenage son could not be found.

I don't usually drive the carpool to the middle school. My regular route includes the elementary and intermediate campuses, but on this day Chase missed his ride home. When that mom-driver reported him AWOL, I told her not to worry. I vaguely remembered talking to him about walking down the street to get a haircut after school.

"I'll swing by and pick him up," I told my friend.

When my nephew, William, and I got to the barber's, William went inside to look for Chase. To my surprise, he wasn't there yet.

"He's probably still talking to his friends at school. Let's go pick him up," I said.

When we got to the school two minutes later, Chase was not in his usual "hang out" spot, so we circled the school, looking for him. No Chase.

"We must have missed him. Let's go back to Milford's," I suggested.

Inside the barbershop there was a room full of junior high boys, but no Chase.

"Go check the bathroom, and I'll see if his backpack is lying around."

We found nothing.

Remembering that he usually carries a little cash in his

pocket, and that he likes gummy bears, I guessed that he made a detour to the candy shop around the corner.

"William, why don't you run over and see if Chase is at Pop's?"

He was back in a flash but found no Chase.

I made another call to the mom who usually brings him home.

"Marcia, would you ask Brittany if she saw Chase after school?" I tried not to sound worried.

Indeed, her daughter had seen him, but he had disappeared before it was time to go. As I circled the building one more time, I spotted some administrators and informed them that my son was missing.

"Has he ever done anything like this before?" they asked.

They obviously did not know my son. I'm under no delusion that he is perfect, but he hates to get in trouble. "Rebel with a cause" he isn't.

"Well, at this age they will do things you hardly expect," they cautioned. Yeah, but Chase?

Now that doubts about my child were planted in my mind I began to think of other possibilities. Maybe he had gotten a ride home with a friend. Not exactly a crime spree, but it would be cause for weekend grounding.

I had remained calm through those forty-five minutes of searching and phone calls, but now I was getting a little worried. As I made my way back to the barber's for the fifth time, I found myself looking down alleys and behind parked cars. Though it was unlikely that someone would mug my 5'9", 142-pound son, vain imaginings were cropping into my mind. That's when Brittany called my cell phone.

"Mrs. Wier? I made some calls and someone saw Chase get in the car with Michael," she reported.

Michael? Michael? Oh, Michael. It was coming back to me. The night before, I had given Chase permission to go home with Michael after school.

The mystery was solved. What a relief! I couldn't find Chase because I was not looking in the place where he had said he would be. My memory had gone AWOL.

Ever wonder why you look for God, but can't find Him anywhere? It could be you're looking in all the wrong places. God cannot be found in crystals, or Mother Earth, or channeling, or even in the great cosmos. He isn't on late-night TV or in the pages of a philosophy book. God can, however, be found exactly where He said He would be.

"Trust in God; trust also in me," Jesus said. *"I am the way and the truth and the life. No one [can find and come] to the Father except through me. If you really knew me, you would know my Father as well"* (Jn 14:1, 6-7, NIV).

If our search is sincere, we have His promise.

"If you seek [for God], he will be found by you" (1 Chr 28:9, NIV).

"For everyone who asks receives; he who seeks finds; and to him who knocks, the door will be opened" (Mt 7:8).

What a relief! God's not lost and He's not hiding. God is right were He said He would be.

My purpose today is to look for God and find Him in His Word.

Psalm 14

Only fools say in their hearts, "There is no God." They are corrupt, and their actions are evil; no one does good! The Lord looks down from heaven on the entire human race; he looks to see if there is even one with real understanding, one who seeks for God. But no, all have turned away from God; all have become corrupt. No one does good, not even one! Will those who do evil never learn? They eat up my people like bread; they wouldn't think of praying to the Lord. Terror will grip them, for God is with those who obey him. The wicked frustrate the plans of the oppressed, but the Lord will protect his people. Oh, that salvation would come from Mount Zion to rescue Israel! For when the Lord restores his people, Jacob will shout with joy, and Israel will rejoice.

Get a (Spiritual) Life

Seeking first things first ...

The Words of Truth reveal that God is ...
_____
_____
_____
_____

The Words of Truth promise, warn, or teach me ...
_____
_____
_____
_____

To seek "first His kingdom and righteousness" today I will ...
_____
_____
_____
_____

The "other things" in my day that I must trust God for are ...
_____
_____
_____
_____

One of God's purposes that He has shown me in my day is ...
_____
_____
_____

Day 13
Running on Empty

It came. Just like the book title, but instead of Alexander, it was "Kim and the Terrible, Horrible, No Good, Very Bad Day."

I should have known it was going to be that way when the alarm rattled me awake an hour earlier than usual, but I had to set it that early. Not only did I have to get three kids to school, but also I had to take my daughter to the hospital to x-ray her broken arm in anticipation of removing her cast. Fortunately, my husband rescued the boys from tardy slips by offering to drop them off on his way to work.

I needed every spare moment. After the hospital, I had to report straight to my kids' school to teach the children's chapel lesson, then rush to get to my own Bible study class. At 6:55 A.M. I was scrambling to make sure I had everything I needed. At 7:05, now late, I looked longingly at the coffeepot, wishing I had time for just one cup, and then rushed Hannah to the car. We were told that if we came to the hospital very early we wouldn't have to wait. At 7:15 we were waiting. That's when my daughter started to cry.

"Mom, my back really hurts. Can the doctor look at it while we're here?"

What we thought was a spot of poison ivy had turned into a flaming red patch on her back that got more painful by the day. Since our doctor was just around the corner we decided we would swing by there on our way to school. At 7:45 she was finally getting X rays and at 8:10 I was holding Hannah's hand as she was getting a painful shot of antibiotics at the doctor's office because her poison ivy turned out to be shingles.

I would have comforted her longer, but two hundred children were waiting for me at chapel. So at 8:15 we stopped to put two gallons of gas in the car so we could make it across town, and then skidded into school just as the principal was giving up hope that we would arrive.

As I looked at those sweet smiling faces, I spotted my son Bailey, sitting up front and looking particularly green. As soon as the lesson was over, the principal put him back in my care and insisted I take him and his newly acquired virus home. I wasn't going to Bible study after all. I made it home just in time to take a call from my husband, who didn't feel so good either.

"Oh honey," I urged, "you should stay at work. I'm sure you'll feel better soon."

By the time my son was fed, cared for, and medicated, it was time to drive carpool. By now, I had used my two gallons of gas and my car stalled in the driveway of one of my carpool-ees. Fortunately, they had a full gas can and I was good for another few miles. I made a mental note—always a mistake for me—to fill up as I took my daughter to soccer and before driving twenty-five miles down the highway to the radio station to tape a broadcast for our radio show.

I was about five miles outside of town when I had that thought again. That's where I ran out of gas for the second time in one day. I didn't panic though. I just grabbed my cell phone and dialed my husband. As soon as Tony answered, my phone battery went dead. Now I was a little worried. I tried again—and again. Each time the phone died before the call connected. I got through just once long enough to yell, "Out of gas, in front of the golf course, hurr ...." Silence.

Eventually, he did find me and I arrived at the radio station just in time. Then I made it home just in time to find my daughter crying in pain, my son nauseated, and my husband ready to detail each of his cold symptoms.

See, it really was a terrible, horrible, no good, very bad day. Thank goodness, for days like those God has words like these:

"The Lord preserves the faithful.... Be strong and take heart, all you who hope in the Lord" (Ps 31:23-24, NIV).

"No good thing does he withhold from those whose walk is blameless" (Ps 84:11, NIV).

Take heart! There is no such thing as a "no good day" for those whose trust is in God. You may still have to endure the "terrible," the "horrible," and even the "very bad," but certainly never a "no good day."

My purpose today is to expect God's goodness in the midst of my trials.

Psalm 27:1-6, 13-14

The Lord is my light and my salvation—so why should I be afraid? The Lord protects me from danger—so why should I tremble? When evil people come to destroy me, when my enemies and foes attack me, they will stumble and fall. Though a mighty army surrounds me, my heart will know no fear. Even if they attack me, I remain confident. The one thing I ask of the Lord—the thing I seek most—is to live in the house of the Lord all the days of my life, delighting in the Lord's perfections and meditating in his Temple. For he will conceal me there when troubles come; he will hide me in his sanctuary. He will place me out of reach on a high rock. Then I will hold my head high, above my enemies who surround me. At his Tabernacle I will offer sacrifices with shouts of joy, singing and praising the Lord with music.... Yet I am confident that I will see the Lord's goodness while I am here in the land of the living. Wait patiently for the Lord. Be brave and courageous. Yes, wait patiently for the Lord.

Get a (Spiritual) Life

Seeking first things first ...

The Words of Truth reveal that God is ...

_____
_____
_____

The Words of Truth promise, warn, or teach me ...

_____
_____
_____
_____

To seek "first His kingdom and righteousness" today I will ...

_____
_____
_____
_____

The "other things" in my day that I must trust God for are ...

_____
_____
_____
_____

One of God's purposes that He has shown me in my day is ...

_____
_____
_____
_____

Day 14
Roll Again

What a day! I was behind on the mortgage, my taxes were due, and I was forced to file bankruptcy. On top of that, I made a bad move that landed me in jail. I might still be there today, if I hadn't rolled doubles.

Since I was a kid, I have had hope that one day I'd be a winner in the risky game of Monopoly. After all, my chances are as good as anyone else's. We all start on the same Go square, with the same $1,500, seeking the same objective: "to become the wealthiest player through buying, renting, and selling property." Scientific probability alone says that I should have won at least one game in all those years. So much for science.

Even now, playing with my own children, my odds haven't improved. Last time we played, I was true to form, starting the game with a roll that landed me in the Income Tax Due space. From there I visited Uncle Billy in the clink, and then was directed by Community Chest to pay each player $50. They, of course, could use the money because while I had floundered, they had bought up all the real estate.

By the time I made it around the board, the only property I was able to buy were Baltic and Mediterranean, which based on their value, are in a flood zone, behind the city dump, next to an airport. Things were not looking good for me. Two more times around the board and my fate was sealed. Defeat was just a matter of time, a fact that did not go

Get a (Spiritual) Life

unnoticed by the competition.

"Mom, you really stink at this game, don't you?"

Suddenly my objective changed. Forget the wealth; how was I going to keep from getting skunked by three snotty-nosed kids? I needed a new strategy. Option one was: Let me win or you go to bed early. Option two: Create a diversion whenever you owe money.

"Hey, Bailey, did you see the monkey in that tree? Go ahead and roll, Chase."

With luck, the landlord wouldn't notice my man until it was too late to collect. My preference was option three: Find an excuse to quit. I had lost all hope of winning anyway. The most exciting thing that had happened by that point was that I had drawn a card declaring me the second-place winner of a beauty contest. The $10 prize actually doubled my cash holdings. Who could blame me for wanting out? My son, that's who.

"You can't quit, Mom. Things could turn around. Look, you're about to pass Go and collect $200," Chase said encouragingly. "Then you'll have enough to pay me when you land on my railroad again."

Spoken like a guy who owned the whole board. But what motivated me to stick it out was my daughter's attitude. With no more assets than I had, she was determined to finish the game. With eight-year-old wisdom she explained, "Daddy always says you only lose if you're a quitter."

The apostle Paul would have liked playing Monopoly with Hannah. He had the same attitude about the uncertain and risky game of life. Sometimes the dice went his way, and sometimes he drew the "go to jail" card, but still he said, *"I have learned to be content whatever the circumstances. I know what it is to be in need, and I know what it is to have plenty. I have learned the secret of being content in any and every situation, whether well fed or hungry, whether living in plenty or in want. I can do everything through him who gives me strength"* (Phil 4:11-13, NIV).

Maybe he found contentment because his objective was never to be a winner. He knew his reward would come simply by not being a quitter.

"I have fought the good fight, I have finished the race, I have kept the faith. Now there is in store for me the crown of righteousness, which the Lord, the righteous Judge, will award to me on that day—and not only to me, but also to all who have longed for his appearing" (2 Tm 4:7-8, NIV).

That is great news for those of us who feel like the dice don't always roll our way in life. More often than not, we pay penalties, we're sent back three spaces, and we land in places we don't really want to be. If our main goal is to stay on easy street, we might feel defeated. But if our goal, like Paul's and Hannah's, is simply to finish the race with faith, then the circumstances in which we find ourselves are not what determine our victory.

The real winners in the game of life are the ones who just keep moving forward with God. Eventually, they will get the prize.

My purpose today isn't to win, but to finish what God has called me to.

Psalm 146

Praise the Lord! Praise the Lord, I tell myself. I will praise the Lord as long as I live. I will sing praises to my God even with my dying breath. Don't put your confidence in powerful people; there is no help for you there. When their breathing stops, they return to the earth, and in a moment all their plans come to an end. But happy are those who have the God of Israel as their helper, whose hope is in the Lord their God. He is the one who made heaven and earth, the sea, and everything in them. He is the one who keeps every promise forever, who gives justice to the oppressed and food to the hungry. The Lord frees the prisoners. The Lord opens the eyes of the blind. The Lord lifts the burdens of those bent beneath their loads. The Lord loves the righteous. The Lord protects the foreigners among us. He cares for the orphans and widows, but he frustrates the plans of the wicked. The Lord will reign forever. O Jerusalem, your God is King in every generation! Praise the Lord!

Get a (Spiritual) Life

Seeking first things first ...

The Words of Truth reveal that God is ...
_____
_____
_____

The Words of Truth promise, warn, or teach me ...
_____
_____
_____
_____

To seek "first His kingdom and righteousness" today I will ...
_____
_____
_____
_____

The "other things" in my day that I must trust God for are ...
_____
_____
_____
_____

One of God's purposes that He has shown me in my day is ...
_____
_____
_____
_____

Day 15
Pilot to Co-Pilot

Dateline (Denver)—Unaware of the danger, passengers of flight 774 remained calm as a near miss in the Colorado skies could have cost them their lives. Instead, hundreds were spared by the skill of their attentive pilots.

The incident began normally. As the plane taxied on the runway, the flight attendant demonstrated safety features in case of a midair catastrophe. I, for one, doubted that my seat floatation device would save me if we hit a mountain range, but I noted the exits anyway.

Upon completing her vivid description of cabin decompression and dropping oxygen bags, she invited us to put on our headphones and relax. We could choose pop music, news, or reggae, or we could tune in to the cockpit transmissions of our flight.

I decided to keep tabs on the captain. My fellow passengers, however, seemed content with their crossword puzzles and magazines. They were probably right not to worry, but I was already tuned in, so I listened.

"Uh, 774, there will be a short delay while we wait for a push back crew to assist you."

"Tower, this is 774. Roger that."

Eventually we were cleared for take-off. My imagination went a little overboard picturing the pilot and co-pilot in the cockpit. It sounded like such fun. Did they turn their hats backward and high five each other when they got the

Get a (Spiritual) Life

go-ahead? I decided to listen a little longer.

"Denver, this is 774. What can we expect in turbulence?"

"Well, 774, that depends on who you ask." *Excuse me,* I thought, *wasn't he just asking you?* "You'll hear from light to chop, or possibly chop to strong."

"Roger, Denver. We will ask around, over."

I didn't have to wonder long who else he would find to ask at 35,000 feet.

"This is Bravo 1074. Go ahead 774."

"Yeah. How is the turbulence at 35?"

"You've got light to chop ahead, 774. It's a little bumpy. Over."

How did that flight attendant say those floatation straps worked? Just as we began to encounter some of that light-to-chop turbulence, we switched to the Albuquerque tower. That's when my stomach bounced into my throat.

"7-7-4. We are unable to raise flight 623 at this time. We need you to drop to 31,000 feet or go up to 37. Which do you prefer?"

I preferred that they find the missing aircraft. What if he decided to go down to 31,000 feet at the same time we did? I looked around the plane but no one else seemed to be listening. I was the only one privy to the midair crisis we were experiencing. Others were working on their laptops, thumbing through magazines, and munching pretzels. Should I alert them or let them enjoy their last few panic-free moments?

I decided to spare them the terror as I prayed silently, waiting for news from the tower, or a sudden free-falling sensation. Meanwhile, back on the radio ... "Tower, this is 774. I have visual contact on that traffic. Requesting 10 degree move left."

Move already. *Move!*

"Roger 774. Please adjust 10 degrees left and maintain current altitude."

Ten degrees? Were we just 10 degrees from that sweet by and by? The people around me had no idea how close they had come to making the evening news. But I knew. And later, when we safely disembarked in Dallas, while others simply passed our pilot with a nod, I made eye contact and heartily thanked the captain for his unseen efforts made on our behalf.

How much more enlightening would it be if we could listen in to unseen spiritual transmissions? Would we find out that through the course of our day, a multitude of dangers are averted by heavenly intervention? Would we find that there is one ultimate Captain directing our paths and delivering us from hazards, both physical and spiritual?

"He who dwells in the shelter of the Most High will rest in the shadow of the Almighty.... He will cover you with his feathers, and under his wings you will find refuge; his faithfulness will be your shield and rampart.... For he will command his angels concerning you to guard you in all your ways" (Ps 91:1, 4, 11, NIV).

There is no need to panic over unseen danger, or even the hazards we can see. Our God will pilot us with faithfulness from on high and deliver us from the midst of trouble.

My purpose today is to live by faith, not by sight.

Psalm 91

Those who live in the shelter of the Most High will find rest in the shadow of the Almighty. This I declare of the Lord: He alone is my refuge, my place of safety; he is my God, and I am trusting him. For he will rescue you from every trap and protect you from the fatal plague. He will shield you with his wings. He will shelter you with his feathers. His faithful promises are your armor and protection. Do not be afraid of the terrors of the night, nor fear the dangers of the day, nor dread the plague that stalks in darkness, nor the disaster that strikes at midday. Though a thousand fall at your side, though ten thousand are dying around you, these evils will not touch you. But you will see it with your eyes; you will see how the wicked are punished. If you make the Lord your refuge, if you make the Most High your shelter, no evil will conquer you; no plague will come near your dwelling. For he orders his angels to protect you wherever you go. They will hold you with their hands to keep you from striking your foot on a stone. You will trample down lions and poisonous snakes; you will crush fierce lions and serpents under your feet! The Lord says, "I will rescue those who love me. I will protect those who trust in my name. When they call on me, I will answer; I will be with them in trouble. I will rescue them and honor them. I will satisfy them with a long life and give them my salvation."

Get a (Spiritual) Life

Seeking first things first ...

The Words of Truth reveal that God is ...

_____
_____
_____
_____

The Words of Truth promise, warn, or teach me ...

_____
_____
_____
_____

To seek "first His kingdom and righteousness" today I will ...

_____
_____
_____
_____

The "other things" in my day that I must trust God for are ...

_____
_____
_____
_____

One of God's purposes that He has shown me in my day is ...

_____
_____
_____

Day 16
Too Many Variables

There are only two kinds of people in this world—math people and English people. I am proof that "never the twain shall meet." That's right, I am an English person.

That means I do not understand terms like associative properties and equilateral triangle. Isn't that somewhere near Bermuda? Nor do I understand the principle that mathematics is different from algebra, algebra is different from geometry, and geometry is different from calculus. And what's that pi thing about? Everyone knows you can get more than 3.1459 slices out of any pie.

Math is just too legalistic for me. You are either right or you are wrong. Where is the compromise? Where is the ideological discussion? Never once did I hear a math teacher ask, "What do you think the writer of this equation was trying to say to us?"

I knew very early that I was not a math person. Thankfully, when I was in school 66 percent was a passing grade. In college I was forced to pursue a liberal arts degree because it required only math for elementary teachers. Even that was a challenge for me. That's how I ended up in journalism. Here, we are all English people, who generally agree that math folks ought to get a life. Unfortunately, if we don't take at least one of them to lunch with us, we won't have anyone who can divide the ticket.

It's ironic, then, after having arranged my whole life

avoiding math that I would find myself at the kitchen table working on my son's junior high pre-algebra homework. In all those years not much had changed. Instead of me helping him, he was trying to explain it to me.

"OK, Mom, 'x' in this formula is a variable. That means it's an unknown factor. The problem can't be solved until we find out what that variable is—that's the value." I tried to keep up, but I was distracted wondering what happened to the sentence from which all those x's had come.

"Mom, look, we have to figure out what to replace the unknown variable with so that we can get the right outcome. Once you do that, the problem is solved."

I listened intently. With two more children waiting in the wings, I knew I would see this again. Still, understanding was difficult for my limited English brain. I decided to employ a literary device to help me grasp the principle behind the problem. I used symbolism to make the math representative of something more tangible.

"OK," I began slowly. "Let's say that the math problem was really just—my life." I could see his math brain shutting down. "It's full of things I can see and even control, like those numbers there. Right?" No answer. "But then there are also some unknown factors that I don't know about yet and can't control." Glazed eyes stared back. "Those are like the 'x' in the formula. The problem is, then, how do I replace those unknown variables with something of value so that I can be sure I get the right outcome? I've got it! I understand now! The answer to 'x' is God."

At that, he gave up and left the room. I, on the other hand, was excited. I had discovered a revolutionary formula, not for math, but for life. It goes like this: The known variables that I can control in my life + the unknown variables that only God can factor perfectly in my life = an outcome that is in His hands to give me hope and bring God glory. That is a formula God has been working for a long time.

"For I know the plans that I have for you, declares the Lord, plans for your welfare and not for calamity, to give you a future and a hope" (Jer 29:11). *"God's purpose was that we who were the first to trust in Christ should praise our glorious God"* (Eph 1:12).

In this life, the only constant that can replace the uncertainty of the unknown is God. Plugging in the value of His sovereignty over things we cannot control is often the only way to find answers and meaning in the midst of life's problems.

I may never understand the principles behind the world of mathematics, but I can understand the principle that all the unknowns in my life are in the hands of a sovereign God who loves me and knows how to work them for the best possible outcome. It's the principle of the God factor.

My purpose today is to factor God into the things that I cannot control.

Psalm 29

Give honor to the Lord, you angels; give honor to the Lord for his glory and strength. Give honor to the Lord for the glory of his name. Worship the Lord in the splendor of his holiness. The voice of the Lord echoes above the sea. The God of glory thunders. The Lord thunders over the mighty sea. The voice of the Lord is powerful; the voice of the Lord is full of majesty. The voice of the Lord splits the mighty cedars; the Lord shatters the cedars of Lebanon. He makes Lebanon's mountains skip like a calf and Mount Hermon to leap like a young bull. The voice of the Lord strikes with lightning bolts. The voice of the Lord makes the desert quake; the Lord shakes the desert of Kadesh. The voice of the Lord twists mighty oaks and strips the forests bare. In his Temple everyone shouts, "Glory!" The Lord rules over the floodwaters. The Lord reigns as king forever. The Lord gives his people strength. The Lord blesses them with peace.

Get a (Spiritual) Life

Seeking first things first ...

The Words of Truth reveal that God is ...
_____
_____
_____
_____

The Words of Truth promise, warn, or teach me ...
_____
_____
_____
_____

To seek "first His kingdom and righteousness" today I will ...
_____
_____
_____
_____

The "other things" in my day that I must trust God for are ...
_____
_____
_____

One of God's purposes that He has shown me in my day is ...
_____
_____
_____

Day 17
Who Me?

Never in a million years would my ninth-grade gym teacher believe that her only D gym student became a girls' P.E. coach. It has been an amazing transformation. If we weren't talking about me, I wouldn't believe it myself.

There is no bigger oxymoron than "Coach Kim." I don't like to sweat. I know little about sports. I can't tell the difference between running shoes and sneakers. And as far as I'm concerned, cross trainers are people who go to seminary. So what possessed me to accept a position to coach girls' P.E. at my children's school for an entire year?

It wasn't long before I was asking the same question. I had agreed to meet Coach Callahan, the boys' gym teacher, a few days before school started to clean out the equipment room. Prepared for manual labor, I dressed in a ball cap, a pair of old shorts, and a shirt that I didn't mind ruining. Both were stained and a little wrinkled, perfect for a workday. Not so perfect for a schoolwide teacher workday.

Coach Callahan neglected to tell me that all the teachers would be present, wearing matching embroidered pant suits, perfectly starched blouses, and my favorite, a little Capri number with beaded fringe. You'll remember, I was wearing wrinkled, stained shorts.

I was seriously questioning if I had made the right choice. (And I'm sure I wasn't the only one.) After all, it wasn't just my poor taste in clothes and lack of experience that brought my qualifications into doubt. There was also the matter of my less than impressive past.

I was the only student in ninth grade to flunk P.E. I always brought up the rear in laps. My chin-up record could be counted on one hand. I was the last girl picked by team captains, and not even a Twinkie bribe could get me a partner in bowling. I was even a bench warmer in square dancing. Truthfully, I preferred it that way. In fact, I liked the bench so much, often I wouldn't dress out, knowing I'd be sent to my favorite spot on the bleachers. I not only avoided sweating that way, I could also bypass that whole communal locker room experience, a set-up I feel sure contributed to my lifelong aversion to athletics.

In light of my past failings, it is amazing that I would volunteer to endure ninty-five-degree heat to lead elementary kids in the pursuit of physical fitness, the very thing I have spent my life circumventing. For Pete's sake, I don't even go to the end of the driveway to get the mail without the aid of my son's scooter.

How can I explain, then, this amazing change of heart? There is only one explanation. I love those kids and wanted to contribute to their lives. I'm a realist, though. Love alone would not make me capable. I owe that to Coach Callahan. Her experience and knowledge enabled me to do things I otherwise could not have done. She provided the resources and help that turned this P.E. drop-out into a P.E. professional—in the loosest sense of the word, of course. Together we challenged kids, trained them, and helped them to grow in character as well as stature. It was one of the greatest experiences of my life.

Nothing in my past would have foretold my position as coach. In fact, it would have seemed inconceivable, almost as inconceivable as a person's unlikely transformation from enemy of God into child of God.

Looking back, there is really nothing in our past that qualifies believers for the position we enjoy today in the kingdom of God. Exactly. As Paul rightly said,

"I am not worthy to be called an apostle [because of my past.] But whatever I am now, it is all because God poured out his special favor on me—and not without results ... yet it was not I but God who was working through me by his grace.... The important thing is that you believed what we preached to you" (1 Cor 15:9-11).

Paul didn't let his feelings of unworthiness keep him from serving with all his might. Neither did he think that anything he accomplished for God was the result of his own great efforts. Instead, to the amazement of those who knew him, and probably even to Paul, God worked through his unqualified life to build the kingdom of God.

Never in a million years would you believe you could qualify to coach others in faith? God has a position available for someone just like you!

My purpose today is to follow God, regardless of the past.

Psalm 8

O Lord, our Lord, the majesty of your name fills the earth! Your glory is higher than the heavens. You have taught children and nursing infants to give you praise. They silence your enemies who were seeking revenge. When I look at the night sky and see the work of your fingers—the moon and the stars you have set in place—what are mortals that you should think of us, mere humans that you should care for us? For you made us only a little lower than God, and you crowned us with glory and honor. You put us in charge of everything you made, giving us authority over all things—the sheep and the cattle and all the wild animals, the birds in the sky, the fish in the sea, and everything that swims the ocean currents. O Lord, our Lord, the majesty of your name fills the earth!

Get a (Spiritual) Life

Seeking first things first ...

The Words of Truth reveal that God is ...

_____
_____
_____
_____

The Words of Truth promise, warn, or teach me ...

_____
_____
_____
_____

To seek "first His kingdom and righteousness" today I will ...

_____
_____
_____
_____

The "other things" in my day that I must trust God for are ...

_____
_____
_____

One of God's purposes that He has shown me in my day is ...

_____
_____
_____

Day 18
While You Were Sleeping

I love to go to sleep at night—and not just because I am generally comatose by the end of the day. I love to sleep because I love to dream. When my head hits the pillow I embark on wonderful, and sometimes bizarre, adventures. I can't control what dreams will come, but they are always larger than life.

My son Bailey has inherited my late-night imagination. He often spends the first few minutes of the morning recounting his midnight adventures. Recently, he was troubled by one of his dreams.

"Mom, I dreamed I was at Six Flags. While we were walking to the next roller coaster I saw this booth where you could adopt things that train you to be a good parent. I went in to adopt a bird, but Chase took it and adopted it first. When I turned around to get something else, Moses was there. He looked right at me and he said, 'Come and follow me. I will make you a great man with many children.' Mom, I think God was telling me He wants me to be a missionary." Then he confessed, "I want to be a dentist."

He was genuinely concerned. "What do you think I should do?"

Thankful that I had already had a cup of coffee, I offered my best advice. "Well, I guess God can talk to us any way He wants. Sometimes He might even use dreams, but it also could have just been your imagination. Either way, I would talk to God about it. I think I would ask God to help you want to be whatever He wants."

The next day Bailey found me again. "Mom, I prayed about my dream. I really think God wants me to be a missionary." Then he honestly added, "I still really want to be a dentist. Now what do I do?"

"I think you just keep asking God to make your dreams for your life the same as His dreams for your life, so that one day you will wake up and realize the thing you want most is exactly what God wants for you. Who knows," I told him, "maybe you will be a missionary dentist."

Then I told him the story of a young woman named Heather Mercer. When Heather dreamed of her Christian life, her dreams never included 105 days in an Afghan prison. Still, she woke up one day and found that was what God had planned.

I shared with Bailey that in front of a crowd of three thousand people, Heather had explained what it took for her to finally embrace God's dream for her life. She was honest to say that when she was arrested, she just didn't know if she could faithfully endure what was to come. "I told God it was just too hard," she said. "He couldn't want this. He couldn't let me die in prison."

Hours of interrogation. Unsanitary conditions. Bombs exploding. The threat of death hanging over her head. Fear of losing her dreams, and even her life, had stolen her peace and shaken her faith. Surely, she thought, this wasn't really God's best. Then God brought to mind words that would change her forever.

"I tell you the truth, unless a kernel of wheat falls to the ground and dies, it remains only a single seed. But if it dies, it produces many seeds. The man who loves his life will lose it, while the man who hates his life in this world will keep it for eternal life. Whoever serves me must follow me; and where I am, my servant also will be. My Father will honor the one who serves me" (Jn 12:24-26, NIV).

Heather realized that God wasn't just talking about physical life and death. "I knew God meant that I had to die to myself. That's what He wanted. I was so afraid of what might happen there that I really had already lost my life.... I had to die to myself, all that I wanted, and accept all that God had planned for me in order to find my life. God hadn't abandoned me in prison. He was honoring me there by showing Himself in a way I would have never known otherwise, but I had to follow Him."

Bailey thought about that for a minute. "Well, if God has picked me out of four billion other people to go be a missionary, I'll follow Him, but if I get put in prison they probably won't let you come and visit me. Maybe you should start praying."

That is good advice for anyone who wants to follow God.

My purpose today is to let go of my dreams and embrace God's bigger ones.

Psalm 62

I wait quietly before God, for my salvation comes from him. He alone is my rock and my salvation, my fortress where I will never be shaken. So many enemies against one man—all of them trying to kill me. To them I'm just a broken-down wall or a tottering fence. They plan to topple me from my high position. They delight in telling lies about me. They are friendly to my face, but they curse me in their hearts. I wait quietly before God, for my hope is in him. He alone is my rock and my salvation, my fortress where I will not be shaken. My salvation and my honor come from God alone. He is my refuge, a rock where no enemy can reach me. O my people, trust in him at all times. Pour out your heart to him, for God is our refuge. From the greatest to the lowliest—all are nothing in his sight. If you weigh them on the scales, they are lighter than a puff of air. Don't try to get rich by extortion or robbery. And if your wealth increases, don't make it the center of your life. God has spoken plainly, and I have heard it many times: Power, O God, belongs to you; unfailing love, O Lord, is yours. Surely you judge all people according to what they have done.

Get a (Spiritual) Life

Seeking first things first ...

The Words of Truth reveal that God is ...
_____
_____
_____
_____

The Words of Truth promise, warn, or teach me ...
_____
_____
_____
_____

To seek "first His kingdom and righteousness" today I will ...
_____
_____
_____
_____

The "other things" in my day that I must trust God for are ...
_____
_____
_____

One of God's purposes that He has shown me in my day is ...
_____
_____
_____
_____

Day 19
Hitch a Ride

Oh, for the days when choosing your mode of transportation was no more complicated than deciding whether you wanted a covered wagon or an uncovered one. The choice was simple and the focus was on where you were going, not how you were going to get there.

I know all too well the importance of making a good choice. Three years ago we leased a large sport utility vehicle so that on the way to where we were going, we could have as much room as possible. I didn't take into consideration just how much gas it would take to keep that monster on the go, and go we did. In thirty-six months, I logged 75,000 miles. You can do the math at only fourteen miles to the gallon. In addition, I was way over my allotted mileage limit, requiring an additional $3,000 in penalties when the lease expired.

I was not anxious to make another car commitment. Instead, I spent an entire summer driving my husband's Jeep (which, by the way, rides about like a covered wagon). He went back to driving our old truck. There were just a few problems with this arrangement. First, we are a family of five and the Jeep is a vehicle for four. Second, Jeeps are made for people dressed in blue jeans or hunting clothes. There is no graceful way to hike up a skirt and climb behind the wheel. I have mooned many in our small community. Finally, after three months, my husband wanted his Jeep back.

So, once again we needed to buy a wagon. With my driving

only increasing day by day, fourteen miles per gallon just wasn't acceptable anymore. This time, gas mileage had to be more of an issue than either style or comfort. That meant an SUV was out. The problem, though, was seating. With three kids and a carpool, a sedan just wouldn't do the trick. I had to face the harsh reality that we were talking about a minivan.

Minivans are nice, respectable vehicles. It's just that I have done the minivan thing. For eight years, when my children were babies, toddlers, and preschoolers, we lived in a van with its fold-down car seats, pockets for toys and stale fries, cup holders filled with sticky goop, and Play-Doh ground into the carpet. I didn't want another van—but I did want twenty-six miles to the gallon. Begrudgingly, I went to test drive the mommy-mobile. It was comfortable. It was fuel-efficient. It was affordable. It was a van. Still, it met every need we had, so I left the details in my husband's hands.

To my surprise, two days and three hundred miles after moving into my new red covered wagon, I had bonded with my van. It helps me get where I am going better than any car I've owned. It gets phenomenal gas mileage, taking me further without stopping. Its ride is smooth and quiet, something any mom can appreciate, even for a few minutes. It even tells me what direction I'm going (right and wrong) and how long it has taken me to get there. I can even get in wearing a dress without causing a public scandal. And best of all, it tells me how far I can go on the amount of gas I have left. (Remember, I'm the one who ran out of gas twice in the same day—in the same car!) Like never before, with all of these things taken care of, I can focus on where I am going, rather than how I am going to get there.

Grace is God's minivan. It is the trustworthy vehicle He provides so that we can focus on where we are going, rather than on how to get there.

"For by grace you have been saved through faith, and this not from yourselves, it is the [ride] from God—not by works, so that no one can boast ... remember that previously you were separated from Christ ... without hope, and without God in the world, [unable to find a trustworthy ride]. But now in Christ Jesus, you who once were far away have been brought near through the blood of Christ" (Eph 2:8-13, my additions).

Some don't like the vehicle God chose for our salvation. They would rather have a sturdy work vehicle, or a ride that provides lots of comforts. How much better to take the ride God offers and focus on the road that lies ahead.

My purpose today is to accept God's riches at Christ's expense.

Psalm 40:1-5, 16-17

I waited patiently for the Lord to help me, and he turned to me and heard my cry. He lifted me out of the pit of despair, out of the mud and the mire. He set my feet on solid ground and steadied me as I walked along. He has given me a new song to sing, a hymn of praise to our God. Many will see what he has done and be astounded. They will put their trust in the Lord. Oh, the joys of those who trust the Lord, who have no confidence in the proud, or in those who worship idols. O Lord my God, you have done many miracles for us. Your plans for us are too numerous to list. If I tried to recite all your wonderful deeds, I would never come to the end of them.... But may all who search for you be filled with joy and gladness. May those who love your salvation repeatedly shout, "The Lord is great!" As for me, I am poor and needy, but the Lord is thinking about me right now. You are my helper and my savior. Do not delay, O my God.

Get a (Spiritual) Life

Seeking first things first ...

The Words of Truth reveal that God is ...

_____
_____
_____

The Words of Truth promise, warn, or teach me ...

_____
_____
_____
_____

To seek "first His kingdom and righteousness" today I will ...

_____
_____
_____
_____

The "other things" in my day that I must trust God for are ...

_____
_____
_____
_____

One of God's purposes that He has shown me in my day is ...

_____
_____
_____
_____

Day 20
To Your Battle Stations

When eight kids reside together for a week, there is bound to be dissension. My three children, their three cousins, and two friends have proved this during one summer vacation. All five girls, except one, banded together braiding hair, polishing nails, and dancing to golden oldies. The three boys, joined by one maverick girl, monopolized the computer, the Nintendo, and the snacks.

As their little cliques solidified, competition naturally emerged. Before long, the two groups were staking out territory and base of operations. Eventually, full-fledged kid-war was declared and security measures had to be taken. Both groups secured member loyalty with binding signatures on a document that read, "I pledge not to betray." Chase, William, Lindsay, and Bailey signed first, creating *Team Striker*. Kirstie, Hannah, Katie, and Amy followed suit, officially establishing the *A Team*.

To keep either group from gaining an unfair advantage, the kids decided to hold a summit to hash out ground rules for their war games. When the team leaders emerged from negotiations they had agreed that neither group would engage in sneak attacks, play dirty tricks, or invade the other's base. Beyond that, my son informed me, "Anything goes."

Well, not quite anything. The leaders still had to attend the Mom Summit. I added, "Don't do anything hurtful, messy, or destructive. Toothpaste, shaving cream, and foaming bath soap are banned. And whatever mess you make, you must help clean up." Meeting my demands meant adjusting their battle plans, so both teams were off to strategize. The boys and Lindsay were the first to return with their top-secret campaign of annoyance.

Reading it, I discovered two important things. First, I would have to supervise these attacks, and second, my son needed help with spelling. This was the list:

"Oure Plans: TP their room, Freeze underwhere, Hands in warm water, Freeze shirts, String roome."

Putting the girls' hands in warm water as they slept was voted out when I explained that if it achieved the desired results the boys would have to change the bed sheets. I vetoed over the string idea for fear someone would get strangled, but approved toilet papering the room. I figured even if the toilet paper wrapped around someone's neck, two-ply wasn't strong enough to choke anyone. As for freezing sundry clothing, I required only that they be clean before going in my freezer.

The girls' plan was similar, but with a few added surprises. They, too, wanted to wrap the enemy's room, but also to mummify the boys in TP and tattoo each one's body with washable markers.

I agreed to help by waking each team while the other slept. At 1 A.M. Lindsay and the boys were roused. They crisscrossed the girls' room with toilet paper, hung Barbie from the ceiling fan, stole the tattoo idea, and froze clean underwear, all while the girls slept soundly. They were back in bed in fifteen minutes.

Get a (Spiritual) Life

At 5 A.M. the girls reciprocated and got the last word by leaving a message on the boys' bedroom window. Scrawled in Passion Pink lipstick they declared *Girls rule—Boys drool.*

Two hours later the house awoke to feigned outrage, laughter, and promises of revenge. Then everyone who made the mess cleaned it up and I had a cup of coffee.

Wouldn't it be great if we could all handle our personal battles the same way? First, we could get a commitment from our family and friends to stand with us and never betray us. Then we would agree on ground rules to keep everything fair. No one could play dirty by saying one thing but doing another. Sneak attacks, like gossiping, would be forbidden, and no one would be allowed to invade another's feelings. But best of all, each of us would have to stick around to clean up the mess our attacks make in someone else's life. Imagine how that one alone would change most of our strategies for getting even and putting people in their places.

It all sounds similar to God's plan for handling dissension among Christians: *"There should be no division in the body.... If one part suffers, every part suffers with it; if one part is honored, every part rejoices with it. Now you are the body of Christ, and each one of you is part of it"* (1 Cor 12:25-27, NIV).

When believers reside in God's family, there is bound to be dissension. But when His children adjust their battle plans to meet His demands, empathy replaces enmity, and restoration replaces revenge. Is this part of your strategy?

My purpose today is to resolve differences, not prepare for war.

Psalm 133

How wonderful it is, how pleasant, when brothers live together in harmony! For harmony is as precious as the fragrant anointing oil that was poured over Aaron's head, that ran down his beard and onto the border of his robe. Harmony is as refreshing as the dew from Mount Hermon that falls on the mountains of Zion. And the Lord has pronounced his blessing, even life forevermore.

Get a (Spiritual) Life

Seeking first things first ...

The Words of Truth reveal that God is ...
_____
_____
_____
_____

The Words of Truth promise, warn, or teach me ...
_____
_____
_____
_____

To seek "first His kingdom and righteousness" today I will ...
_____
_____
_____
_____

The "other things" in my day that I must trust God for are ...
_____
_____
_____

One of God's purposes that He has shown me in my day is ...
_____
_____
_____

Day 21
Wanted

When you go to the post office, don't be surprised if you find my picture posted on the wall next to all the other fugitives. I am an outlaw.

It all started so innocently. With my van packed to the rafters with supplies for our retreat, a friend and I left our cumulative five children and two husbands and started our road trip. This time we were traveling to Houston to speak to a women's group about taking the stress out of Christmas, even while our own to-do lists remained undone. We had laundry piled on the bed waiting to be folded, no food in the refrigerator, birthday party gifts not purchased, Sunday Bible verses unlearned, soccer socks still missing ... but time was up. We had to get on the road so we could tell others how to overcome stress.

To be honest, the least stressful place for me is in my car. My philosophy has always been, "when the going gets tough, the tough hit the road—and they don't tell anyone where they're going."

You couldn't call this trip an escape, though. We were on our way to do ministry and we were running late. Surely that justified a slight increase in my speed, so I was cruising down the highway at seventy-five miles per hour. I did not see this as a problem. After all, if the speed limit was seventy miles per hour, I was practically right on the mark. When blue and white lights began flashing behind me, I just couldn't imagine

Get a (Spiritual) Life

why a state trooper would want to pull me over, but when I changed lanes he stayed right on my tail. I indulged him in his mistake and pulled over anyway.

"Ma'am," he said with his most serious expression, "do you know what you did wrong?"

A long list flashed through my mind. Let's see, I didn't change the bunny litter, my checkbook didn't balance this month, I put a red towel in with my husband's white underwear, and I am having bad thoughts about a certain state trooper. I didn't suppose that he meant any of those.

I took a wild guess. "Am I speeding?"

"Ma'am, you were doing seventy-five in a fifty-five mile per hour zone."

I proceeded to discuss with him how he must be mistaken. The last time I had driven to Houston, two years earlier, the speed limit had been seventy miles per hour. I had not received a personal notification of the speed change. This did not sway Mr. Trooper. After an extended time of running a background check on my vehicle and me he began writing my ticket.

"Couldn't I just get a warning this time?" I asked, now much more contrite.

"No, ma'am, but I won't record that this occurred in a construction zone, which would double your fine."

He did, however, ticket me for not having proof of insurance in my vehicle, even though I explained to him that it was a new car and that when the new insurance card arrived I would give it a place of honor in my glove box.

I made the decision then and there that I would contest

this injustice. It was unfair that I should be held to an unreasonable standard without any say. I was going to take it to the judge.

This determination to fight made me a fugitive. It all started with my attitude.

I regarded this man-made law in much the same way that most of us look at God's laws—as if they are mere suggestions for those who are uncomfortable deciding for themselves what's safe and right. Surely they weren't actually meant to be followed! While God does really mean what He says, it is also true that His laws are impossible to follow without fault.

"No one can ever be made right in God's sight by doing what his law commands. For the more we know God's law, the clearer it becomes that we aren't obeying it" (Rom 3:20).

Unlike man's law, the point of God's law was never to master it, but to draw us to the only One who has mastered it for us, Jesus Christ. He didn't just write the law, He fulfilled it completely. Any who miss that mark, even the worst lawbreakers and fugitives, who throw themselves on the mercy of His court, will not be condemned.

The Splendor, Texas, court is another story, however. I'll tell you the rest tomorrow—right after I tell my husband.

My purpose today is to thank my Judge for His mercy, but to love His laws, too.

Psalm 51:1-12, 16-17

Have mercy on me, O God, because of your unfailing love. Because of your great compassion, blot out the stain of my sins. Wash me clean from my guilt. Purify me from my sin. For I recognize my shameful deeds—they haunt me day and night. Against you, and you alone, have I sinned; I have done what is evil in your sight. You will be proved right in what you say, and your judgment against me is just. For I was born a sinner—yes, from the moment my mother conceived me. But you desire honesty from the heart, so you can teach me to be wise in my inmost being. Purify me from my sins, and I will be clean; wash me, and I will be whiter than snow. Oh, give me back my joy again; you have broken me—now let me rejoice. Don't keep looking at my sins. Remove the stain of my guilt. Create in me a clean heart, O God. Renew a right spirit within me. Do not banish me from your presence, and don't take your Holy Spirit from me. Restore to me again the joy of your salvation, and make me willing to obey you.... You would not be pleased with sacrifices, or I would bring them. If I brought you a burnt offering, you would not accept it. The sacrifice you want is a broken spirit. A broken and repentant heart, O God, you will not despise.

Get a (Spiritual) Life

Seeking first things first ...

The Words of Truth reveal that God is ...

_____
_____
_____
_____

The Words of Truth promise, warn, or teach me ...

_____
_____
_____
_____

To seek "first His kingdom and righteousness" today I will ...

_____
_____
_____
_____

The "other things" in my day that I must trust God for are ...

_____
_____
_____

One of God's purposes that He has shown me in my day is ...

_____
_____
_____

Day 22
Throw Away the Key

Crime does not pay. In fact, it can be very costly. As a result of trying to make up a little time on that recent road trip, I was slapped with a speeding ticket.

I resolved that I would not be railroaded by such an injustice. Determined to plead my case to someone more reasonable, I would not plead guilty and pay the ticket. First, I could not afford the hike in insurance that it would cause. More importantly, though, as Americans, what we really can't afford is to compromise our principles. It is wrong to prey on the weaknesses of our citizenry and to willy-nilly hand out tickets without regard to extenuating circumstances. We, the people, should not be responsible for knowing every time some official decides to monkey with the speed limits on the highway. I was caught in the trap of deception and it could not stand. I would fight that ticket for all the inadvertent speeders who were without a voice. I would appeal to the judge and justice would prevail.

It was three weeks later when I remembered how strongly I felt about my crusade. After digging through several piles, I finally found my ticket. Locating the phone number of the municipal court in question, I called to put the wheels of justice in motion. Unfortunately, I found that they were already turning.

After giving my name and pertinent information, I told the clerk, "I should not have gotten a ticket under those circumstances. I would like to speak to the judge and protest."

"Honey," she said, "that's all well and good, but you should have called yesterday. You missed your court date and they have issued a warrant for your arrest."

In that instant, my principles wavered. Speaking for the masses didn't seem as important as the fact that I was a fugitive from the law. I could actually be put in jail over this! Then who'd drive carpool? I was sure I had blown my chance with the judge. It was time to compromise.

If I wanted to avoid arrest and keep the whole ugly incident off my record, the clerk said I would have to overnight a money order for the fine with a notarized copy of my ticket, explaining my intent to take drivers education. It seemed the only way. I would have to fight for principle another day. This one I could not afford, but that didn't mean the compromise was cheap. The fine was $65, the overnight package was $15, the processing fee to the state was $10, and I knew the drivers education class would cost at least $35. After adding it all up, I wondered if the best thing wasn't simply to turn myself in and serve my thirty days. I needed a little rest anyway. Let someone serve meals to me for a change. It could be a great opportunity for prison ministry, with me as the prisoner.

However, pretty sure I would not look good in an orange jumpsuit, I mailed in my fine and found a driving school—and so ended my life of crime. In the end, keeping my freedom was costly, but it was worth the price I had to pay.

In comparison, the price we must pay to win our freedom

from judgment for breaking God's laws is beyond the means of even the most resourceful. If not for the mercy of the Judge Himself, we would forever be prisoners of our own sin. *"God alone made it possible for you to be in Christ Jesus.... He is the one who made us acceptable to God. He made us pure and holy and he gave himself to purchase our freedom"* (1 Cor 1:30).

"God sent him to buy freedom for us who were slaves to the law, so that he could adopt us as his very own children" (Gal 4:5).

"You are trying to find favor with God by what you do or don't do on certain days or months or seasons or years.... I plead with you to live as I do in freedom from these things ... free from the law" (Gal 4:10-12).

"He is so rich in kindness that he purchased our freedom through the blood of his Son, and our sins are forgiven" (Eph 1:7).

Our freedom was costly, but God deemed it worth the price only Christ could pay.

My purpose today is to worship the Lamb who is worthy.

Psalm 113

Praise the Lord! Yes, give praise, O servants of the Lord. Praise the name of the Lord! Blessed be the name of the Lord forever and ever. Everywhere—from east to west—praise the name of the Lord. For the Lord is high above the nations; his glory is far greater than the heavens. Who can be compared with the Lord our God, who is enthroned on high? Far below him are the heavens and the earth. He stoops to look, and he lifts the poor from the dirt and the needy from the garbage dump. He sets them among princes, even the princes of his own people! He gives the barren woman a home, so that she becomes a happy mother. Praise the Lord!

Get a (Spiritual) Life

Seeking first things first ...

The Words of Truth reveal that God is ...
_____
_____
_____
_____

The Words of Truth promise, warn, or teach me ...
_____
_____
_____
_____

To seek "first His kingdom and righteousness" today I will ...
_____
_____
_____
_____

The "other things" in my day that I must trust God for are ...
_____
_____
_____

One of God's purposes that He has shown me in my day is ...
_____
_____
_____

Day 23
Strange Bedfellows

Our peaceful home was turned upside down when my son casually mentioned that he didn't see our pet snake in the laundry room terrarium.

When I opened the cage I realized Bailey was right. The snake wasn't there. It had managed to break out. In the vain hope that it had just escaped, I began tearing the laundry room apart. I looked in drawers and under laundry baskets. I looked in shoes and socks lying on the floor. I searched through cabinets, under the washing machine, behind the hot water heater, and in the clothes hamper. It was gone.

For the first few days I didn't mention the situation to my husband. In the several months that we had owned the snake Tony had never touched it. He hates reptiles. He made it very clear to the kids that if the snake got near him he would reach for the machete first and ask questions later. As often as we teased him about slipping the snake into one of his shoes, we knew he meant business. Snakes give Tony the creeps, and even having it in the laundry room in a cage made him uncomfortable. How would I tell him that the snake was on the loose?

By the way, honey, I practiced, *if you feel something slithering around your feet under the covers at night, don't be afraid.*

Maybe something less ominous: *Honey, the funniest thing happened on the way to the laundry room....*

Get a (Spiritual) Life

Or perhaps a psychological approach: *Honey, you know what they say about having nothing to fear but fear itself....*

Maybe I would just look a little harder. I got a flashlight and searched in and under every piece of furniture downstairs. I even set out some little snake morsels, hoping to entice the critter out of hiding. I soon discovered that was a mistake. The cats were more interested in the little frozen mice snacks than the snake was.

That's when I realized my next problem. The snake was two feet of slithering, wiggling, cat-enticing motion. If one of our three felines found it before we did, the snake would be the snack. Now I had to worry about keeping the snake away from my husband and the cats away from the snake. After a week of all the intrigue I finally broke down and let Tony in on our secret.

"Honey, I don't want you to panic, but the snake has gotten loose and we can't find him, but it's harmless," I added quickly. "If you find him somewhere just back away and call one of the kids. They'll catch it."

He took this news far better than I expected. He didn't move into a hotel or call the exterminator. He simply suggested that for the snake's well being, we find it before he did. Keeping in mind that he graciously put up with the cats, dogs, birds, rabbits, ferret, turtles, tadpoles, frogs, guinea pigs, hamsters, and even the tarantula, I assured him that we would not rest until we had recaptured the one animal that threatened his peace.

After three weeks of searching, I was beginning to doubt that assurance. That's when I caught a glimpse of the snake slithering up inside Tony's favorite chair. What would Tony say about the fact that every time he sat down to enjoy the newspaper or a ball game he was just inches away from one of his greatest fears?

As I recaptured the snake and put it back where it belonged, I convinced myself that Tony didn't need to know all the details. Unfortunately, the kids thought that was the best part of the story and made sure to give him all the particulars. The bottom line, though, was that finally, my husband could rest in peace.

Like Tony, most of us have discovered, that there are many things that can slither through life that threaten to steal our peace. They come in the form of worries, illnesses, stress, troubles of many kinds, even escaped critters. That's why God reminds us of two very important details.

First, *"God himself is our peace,"* not circumstances (Eph 2:14). And Christ said, *"I have told you these things, so that in me you may have peace. In this world you will have trouble. But take heart! I have overcome the world"* (Jn 16:33, NIV).

"Now may the Lord of peace himself continually grant you peace in every circumstance," (2 Thes 3:16) no matter what slinks through your life.

My purpose today is to focus on God, not the unpleasant things slinking through my life.

Psalm 23 (NIV)

The Lord is my shepherd, I shall not be in want. He makes me lie down in green pastures, he leads me beside quiet waters, he restores my soul. He guides me in paths of righteousness for his name's sake. Even though I walk through the valley of the shadow of death, I will fear no evil, for you are with me; your rod and your staff, they comfort me. You prepare a table before me in the presence of my enemies. You anoint my head with oil; my cup overflows. Surely goodness and love will follow me all the days of my life, and I will dwell in the house of the Lord forever.

Get a (Spiritual) Life

Seeking first things first ...

The Words of Truth reveal that God is ...

_____
_____
_____

The Words of Truth promise, warn, or teach me ...

_____
_____
_____
_____

To seek "first His kingdom and righteousness" today I will ...

_____
_____
_____
_____

The "other things" in my day that I must trust God for are ...

_____
_____
_____
_____

One of God's purposes that He has shown me in my day is ...

_____
_____
_____
_____

Day 24
No Hablo Español

A while back I received a flyer advertising a course in Spanish. Because we live in a border state, I thought it would be a good idea to enroll. Then I realized the class conflicted with my daughter's gymnastics, and I didn't feel I should deprive the world of another Nadia or Mary Lou. I came to regret that decision when we hired a man to help with some landscaping.

Mr. Lopez arrived early one weekday morning. My husband, being a native of El Paso, knows a minimal amount of Spanish. He may fracture sentences and mutilate digraphs but the basic message survives. Using this pseudo-Spanish, Tony explained to Mr. Lopez that a pallet of grass sod needed to be moved across the yard. Satisfied that he understood, my husband left for work, assuring Mr. Lopez that I could show him the rest.

Did I mention that I speak virtually no Spanish? I know that *aqua* is water and my pets are *gatos* and *perros*. (We were in business if it started raining cats and dogs.) Likewise, Mr. Lopez spoke no English. Yet he began asking questions right away. I knew it was something about the grass because he kept pointing to it. I concentrated as he said the same phrases over and over. It made no sense. Finally I confessed, "No comprende. No habla Español."

"No Español?" he questioned. "Ahhhhh," he said knowingly. "No English," he finally admitted. Well, I was glad we

Get a (Spiritual) Life

had cleared that up. Now what? If we couldn't agree about the grass, how was I going to explain that the slope on the front lawn needed grading? After more fruitless attempts, I got a rake and demonstrated the task. Understanding flashed across his face. He began shooting words at me excitedly, nodding his head furiously. "Buenos, Buenos," he repeated. I nodded back and soon we were both giddy with the realization that we had communicated. I went inside, confident that Mr. Lopez and I understood one another.

Five minutes later the doorbell rang. Mr. Lopez had a question, something about *aqua*. It was cloudy. Was he worried about rain? Frustrated, he changed the question to *esposo*. In a bizarre game of charades I finally realized he wanted to know when my husband, my *esposo*, would be home. I tried not to take it personally. All I could do was shrug my shoulders.

I was looking for our Spanish-English dictionary when an idea struck me. I know a woman who speaks both English and Spanish. I made a desperate call and she came to translate. I described the work to Irene, who effortlessly explained it to Mr. Lopez. After a few exchanges Irene translated his questions to me. *How high did I want the soil? How far back should he grade? Could I please get him a glass of water?*

What a relief. We were having a conversation, even though neither of us said anything differently. He still spoke Spanish and I spoke only English. The difference was Irene. She was able to take what was a mystery to me and make it clear, something I couldn't do for myself.

How glad I am that the Holy Spirit does that same thing

for us when it comes to understanding God's Word. Because we are natural and He is spiritual, we don't have the capability to comprehend the mysteries of God.

"A natural man does not accept the things of the Spirit of God; for they are foolishness to him, and he cannot understand them, because they are spiritually appraised" (1 Cor 2:14).

Outside of a relationship with Jesus Christ, God's Word is just so much Greek. Frustrated people hear the words yet fail to comprehend the meaning. But, a loving God who desires for all to know Him reaches beyond even His inspired Word: *"Since the creation of the world His invisible attributes, His eternal power and divine nature, have been clearly seen, being understood through what has been made"* (Rom 1:20).

In a pantomime of nature He speaks the truth of His sovereignty that is understandable to anyone who is willing to see. To those who will believe He gives not *"a spirit of the world but the Spirit who is from God, that we may understand what God has freely given us"* (1 Cor 2:12, NIV). When I open God's Word and it seems I'm reading a foreign language, I stop for a refresher course in Holy Spirit 101. Prayerfully, depending on Him as divine translator, I begin to understand the loving encouragement, the guidance, the words of warning and conviction, and the voice that beckons me into an intimate conversation with my Lord and Savior.

Viva el Espiritu Santo!

> My purpose today is to learn from the Holy Spirit what God has to say.

Psalm 63

O God, you are my God; I earnestly search for you. My soul thirsts for you; my whole body longs for you in this parched and weary land where there is no water. I have seen you in your sanctuary and gazed upon your power and glory. Your unfailing love is better to me than life itself; how I praise you! I will honor you as long as I live, lifting up my hands to you in prayer. You satisfy me more than the richest of foods. I will praise you with songs of joy. I lie awake thinking of you, meditating on you through the night. I think how much you have helped me; I sing for joy in the shadow of your protecting wings. I follow close behind you; your strong right hand holds me securely. But those plotting to destroy me will come to ruin. They will go down into the depths of the earth. They will die by the sword and become the food of jackals. But the king will rejoice in God. All who trust in him will praise him, while liars will be silenced.

Get a (Spiritual) Life

Seeking first things first ...

The Words of Truth reveal that God is ...
_____
_____
_____

The Words of Truth promise, warn, or teach me ...
_____
_____
_____
_____

To seek "first His kingdom and righteousness" today I will ...
_____
_____
_____
_____

The "other things" in my day that I must trust God for are ...
_____
_____
_____
_____

One of God's purposes that He has shown me in my day is ...
_____
_____
_____
_____

Day 25
Cajun Country

Out of sight, out of mind. That was my husband's approach to a New Year's weekend. He was whisking me off to a surprise getaway, leaving behind his parents to manage six grandchildren, our friends' two children, three cats, and a new puppy (with my sister-in-law's help.) "I've taken care of everything," he said again, as he closed the car door. "Don't give them another thought." But as we drove out of sight, they were not out of my mind.

My surprise was a trip to New Orleans. My husband had gotten four tickets on a Mississippi River fireworks cruise on New Year's Eve and four tickets to the Sugar Bowl on New Year's Day. "The Sugar Bowl. Oh, honey, you shouldn't have," I said in stunned amazement.

By the nature of the gift, you might assume I'm a football fan, or maybe a Texas A&M alumnus, since they were playing Ohio State. I'm neither. So what possessed my husband to plan such a trip for me? I couldn't bring myself to ask. It didn't really matter. I was going to New Orleans with my husband and our good friends Deborah and William. So, I'd sit through a football game. That's a small price to pay for such a big gesture.

The six-hour drive was filled with laughter, hits from the eighties, and phone calls home. Chaos hadn't broken out yet, but one child was homesick and the puppy had soiled the carpet—nothing to turn back for. We checked into the hotel,

Get a (Spiritual) Life

and then walked to the dock to board the riverboat. We were starving, but decided that at $68 a ticket they would surely have food on the boat. As soon as we left the dock for our two-hour cruise, the captain said, "We regret that there will be no fireworks display on the 'Mississippi Fireworks Cruise.' The truck carrying fireworks exploded earlier this evening."

"Well, we can still enjoy the ride and have something to eat," my friend said. As if on cue, a steward placed a cup of Chex mix in front of us.

"Excuse me," I said. "Is there a buffet or an appetizer table?"

"No ma'am. Just Chex mix."

In desperation we headed for the gift shop in search of more substantial food. We returned with two Snickers, a bag of M&M's, and a deck of cards. To the sound of Cajun music in the background, we played stupid card games, laughed, and ate Chex mix and chocolate until the new year arrived.

Early the next morning, the phone rang. My sister-in-law asked my friend, "Does your daughter normally wheeze all night?" Apparently, the cats' hair was to blame, but it was nothing antihistamines couldn't cure, so we were off to explore the French Quarter. There we saw street dancers, parades, and musicians. We lunched on Cajun cuisine and had dessert in a turn-of-the-century courtyard. Then we shopped at the mall built under our hotel. That's when the first "panic call" came.

"Do you know where your vaporizer is?" My mother-in-law was frantic.

My niece was also having an allergic reaction to cat hair,

Get a (Spiritual) Life

and they had left her medicine in Houston. After two more calls, the vaporizer was located, but not a pharmacy to fill her prescription.

"I guess I should take her to the emergency room," said my sister-in-law.

Guilt hung heavy on my cat-loving heart. I was determined to find her medicine. As everyone waited to go to the football game, I made several calls back home. Finally, I reached a pharmacist friend who could help.

"Now, you go ahead and have a good time," my mother-in-law said. "Don't worry about us, we're managing. By the way, your puppy has severe diarrhea, but don't worry about that now." Would they ever visit us again? We left for the game.

Our seats were on the forty-five yard line—on the Ohio side. Not a problem for me, but our friends were A&M alumni surrounded by Ohio fans. It was a long walk back to the hotel after their alma mater lost. Still, it was our last night together, so we enjoyed late-night coffee and still more laughs together.

We returned home the next day to one caged puppy, a very noisy house, and two frazzled grandparents. We had our belated family Christmas that night, and by first light, they were all on their way home.

You might be tempted to think that my surprise getaway was disappointing—a river cruise with no fireworks, a football game I wasn't interested in, and chaos at home. I guess I could have been disappointed if I had been measuring the content of the gift instead of the context. How it was given, though, far outweighed what was given. My husband sacrificed to give me a trip. He planned it himself, adding details here and there that evidenced his love. And my in-laws graciously helped so I could enjoy all that he had planned. In that context, it was an abundantly generous gift that I would not exchange.

Proverbs 15:17 says it like this: *"Better is a dish of vegetables where love is, than a fattened calf with hatred."*

When any action, big or small, is motivated by love, only one response is an option: a grateful heart.

My purpose today is to be thankful and content with God's blessings and the gestures of others.

Psalm 118:1, 19-29

Give thanks to the Lord, for he is good! His faithful love endures forever.... Open for me the gates where the righteous enter, and I will go in and thank the Lord. Those gates lead to the presence of the Lord, and the godly enter there. I thank you for answering my prayer and saving me! The stone rejected by the builders has now become the cornerstone. This is the Lord's doing, and it is marvelous to see. This is the day the Lord has made. We will rejoice and be glad in it. Please, Lord, please save us. Please, Lord, please give us success. Bless the one who comes in the name of the Lord. We bless you from the house of the Lord. The Lord is God, shining upon us. Bring forward the sacrifice and put it on the altar. You are my God, and I will praise you! You are my God, and I will exalt you! Give thanks to the Lord, for he is good! His faithful love endures forever.

Get a (Spiritual) Life

Seeking first things first ...

The Words of Truth reveal that God is ...

_____
_____
_____

The Words of Truth promise, warn, or teach me ...

_____
_____
_____
_____

To seek "first His kingdom and righteousness" today I will ...

_____
_____
_____
_____

The "other things" in my day that I must trust God for are ...

_____
_____
_____
_____

One of God's purposes that He has shown me in my day is ...

_____
_____
_____
_____

Day 26
Mint Julep, Anyone?

It was recently brought to my attention that while I have lived in the South for thirty-five of my forty years I am, regrettably, not a true Southern belle. To a true southerner, I am, and always will be, a newcomer.

I gave myself away recently to some friends, who looked aghast when I teased about wearing white shoes on the first day of spring, rather than waiting until Easter. Truly concerned for my reputation, Linda persuaded me away from that reckless path.

"You absolutely cannot wear white before Easter. That's just too tacky."

And as long as we were on the subject, there were a few other fine points of southern etiquette she thought that I should know. My precious friend pointed out that velvet should never be worn after Valentine's Day (I'm pretty sure I've done that), true southern ladies always wear pantyhose (I never do that), and wearing white shoes *after* Labor Day is as tacky as wearing red to a wedding.

Those few hard and fast rules, however, are just the tip of the iceberg when it comes to the deportment of a true Southern belle. According to my friend, it is also about choosing the right silver pattern, having the ability to give a themed party, never using dark meat in your chicken salad, making sure your shoes and your handbag match, never chewing gum in public, knowing the right casserole to take to a funeral ... and on and on the list goes.

To help me better understand and reform, Linda loaned me a must for all belle wanna-be's, a small handbook titled *A Southern Belle Primer*, by Marylyn Schwartz. In it she explains the mysteries of the Southern belle and the unique society in which they operate.

Ms. Schwartz explains that life for the true belle is a cradle-to-grave quest to keep intact all the traditions and grandeur of the old South matriarchs. Though, of course, the modern belle does not have firsthand knowledge of those days of grace, it is said that if she was born south of the Mason-Dixon line (and she had the right parents) she inherited that super-southern instinct. Heritage, then, according to Ms. Schwartz, is everything. "Southerners never tire of talking about their bloodlines," she says. "In the South, roots mean everything." Especially when it comes to winning a crown.

Having the right bloodlines, in the South, is as good as gold. "A Southern belle is born knowing she is going to be Southern royalty. If her mother was a Queen or Princess ... of the Fiesta or Cotton Carnival, then she knows one day if she ... has a daddy who is willing to ... pay for her royal robes, then she, too, will one day wear a crown."

And though a crown means a great deal to many, Ms. Schwartz quoted one belle as saying about the St. Cecilia Society Ball, a less flashy, but more tasteful event than most, "We don't need jeweled robes and glittering crowns to know that we belong.... If you get an invitation, that is quite enough. It's the same as a royal decree."

After reading the handbook cover to cover, I have no

doubt that there is little chance of my becoming one of those big-haired belles who dyes her shoes to match her gowns and hosts dinner parties for twenty with her Francis I silver. I am hopelessly attached to my sneakers, my dinnerware comes from Target, and when I talk about my roots it is usually because I need to color my hair.

Still, I would put my bloodline up against theirs any day. You see, I, too, have confidence that I am royalty—because I have a Daddy who was willing to pay the price for my royal robes.

"But God demonstrates His own love toward us, in that while we were yet sinners, Christ died for us" (Rom 5:8).

"The Spirit Himself bears witness with our spirit that we are children of God, and if children, heirs also, heirs with God and fellow heirs with Christ" (Rom 8:16-17).

"And remember that the heavenly Father to whom you pray has no favorites when he judges.... God paid a ransom to save you ... and the ransom he paid was not mere gold or silver. He paid for you with the precious life blood of Christ, the sinless, spotless Lamb of God" (1 Pt 1:17-19, NLT).

For anyone willing to accept, the Father Himself sends an invitation that is indeed a royal decree. It reads, "Salvation to all who will believe." It comes with a crown, too, the crown of righteousness waiting in eternity. And who knows, instead of a mansion maybe there will be a plantation in the southern part of heaven.

My purpose today is to remember whose daughter I really am, and seek only His approval.

Psalm 45:1-2, 6-11 (NIV)

My heart is stirred by a noble theme as I recite my verses for the king; my tongue is the pen of a skillful writer. You are the most excellent of men and your lips have been anointed with grace, since God has blessed you forever.... Your throne, O God, will last for ever and ever; a scepter of justice will be the scepter of your kingdom. You love righteousness and hate wickedness; therefore God, your God, has set you above your companions by anointing you with the oil of joy. All your robes are fragrant with myrrh and aloes and cassia; from palaces adorned with ivory the music of the strings makes you glad. Daughters of kings are among your honored women; at your right hand is the royal bride in gold of Ophir. Listen, O daughter, consider and give ear: Forget your people and your father's house. The king is enthralled by your beauty; honor him, for he is your lord.

Get a (Spiritual) Life

Seeking first things first ...

The Words of Truth reveal that God is ...

___

The Words of Truth promise, warn, or teach me ...

___

To seek "first His kingdom and righteousness" today I will ...

___

The "other things" in my day that I must trust God for are ...

___

One of God's purposes that He has shown me in my day is ...

___

Day 27
Cry Me a River

Wouldn't it be wonderful if we had to do only things that we are good at? Only chefs would cook, only CPAs would balance checkbooks, and only gardeners would till the soil. In the real world, though, it's sometimes necessary to tackle the unfamiliar.

We are always in the middle of home improvement projects. To be economical, my husband and I do the work. Generally I see my role as a supervisor. I plan the projects, assign tasks, and monitor the progress. I say things like, "Honey, a little more to the left." "Sweetie, I changed my mind. Could you repaint that blue?" And, "Dear, I've got to run up to the mall. Could you have that done when I get back?" It's an efficient system. I do what I'm good at and Tony does everything else.

In one instance, however, I was forced to abandon my usual post and join the working ranks. Landscape beds needed to be built and Tony had three other projects. There was no choice but for me to do it. This was definitely not a natural fit. I'm known in the plant world as a serial killer, wanted for deaths from a to z (azalea to zinnia.) I don't have a clue about plants, but it had to be done.

I started by drawing the beds on graph paper. I added the bushes and edging and embellished it with colored pencils. It was going pretty well. Next I called a nurseryman to advise me on bed preparation and plant selection. That's when the trouble started. "Oh, ma'am," he said ominously, "you have too much clay in this soil for shrubs."

Get a (Spiritual) Life

Apparently, plants don't like their little feet to stay wet, and clay doesn't absorb water properly. "You will need to bring in several yards of mulch after you till the soil." My helpful husband stayed around just long enough to show me how to run the tiller. From there I was on my own. I fired it up and let it drag me through the beds. An hour later, with one significant burn from the tiller's motor, I was ready to add the mulch. I backed up the truck and, with blistered hands, began shoveling six yards of mulch. By the time I was done I felt satisfied my plants' feet would be high and dry. A week later, under cloudy skies, I planted twenty-two gardenias, seventeen Nandinas, twelve Chrysanthemums, five Wax Leaf Hollies, four Lugustrums, three Red Camellias, two Pyracanthas, and no pear tree. It took several hours to tuck them all into their places. I planted the last four as the rain began to pour.

Soaked, I stood on the porch, admiring my beautiful new plants, the dark rich mulch, and the floating bark. Why was my bark floating? Why was my bed filling up with water? The rain was coming down with such velocity that it was pouring from downspouts into the beds like water from a broken main. Working in the deluge, I tried to dig a trench for the water, but as fast as I could dig, the sides caved in. Sprawled in the grass, I tried to scrape the mudslide back in place, but the current was too strong. Pictures of the Midwest floods flashed in my mind. Nature was going to win. I gave up and went to take a hot shower.

It took more than twenty-four hours for the lake in my yard to drain, leaving a mud hole in its place. Repair work would have to be done. This time I called on a master gardener for advice—my mom. She surmised that I needed to reroute my downspouts, install edging, and add a French drain. I had no experience with any of these, but with her help the job eventually got done.

More often than not, God also calls us to things beyond our natural abilities. To the shy, the command to boldy proclaim the gospel seems impossible. To the natural leader, the command to be a servant seems irrational. To someone wronged, the mandate to love an enemy seems overwhelming. Yet God's Word promises, "all things are possible with God." Is that because as Christians we become superhuman? Not in my case, or in the apostle Paul's, either.

"We are not adequate in ourselves to consider anything as coming from ourselves, but our adequacy is from God, who also made us adequate as servants of a new covenant..." (2 Cor 3:5, NIV).

God's grace shines brightest when we serve out of weakness. God Himself said, *"My grace is sufficient for you, for power is perfected in weakness."* It may not be comfortable and it may not be easy, but we can say, as Paul said, *"Most gladly, therefore, I will rather boast about my weakness, that the power of Christ may dwell in me. Therefore, I am well content with weaknesses,... for Christ's sake; for when I am weak, then I am strong"* (2 Cor 12:9-10).

So, go ahead, serve, shovel, give, proclaim, stay silent, forgive, lead. Trust that God is prepared enough for both of you.

My purpose today is not to turn away from the impossible, but to shine God's power in my weakness.

Psalm 28

O Lord, you are my rock of safety. Please help me; don't refuse to answer me. For if you are silent, I might as well give up and die. Listen to my prayer for mercy as I cry out to you for help, as I lift my hands toward your holy sanctuary. Don't drag me away with the wicked—with those who do evil—those who speak friendly words to their neighbors while planning evil in their hearts.... They care nothing for what the Lord has done or for what his hands have made. So he will tear them down like old buildings, and they will never be rebuilt! Praise the Lord! For he has heard my cry for mercy. The Lord is my strength, my shield from every danger. I trust in him with all my heart. He helps me, and my heart is filled with joy. I burst out in songs of thanksgiving. The Lord protects his people and gives victory to his anointed king. Save your people! Bless Israel, your special possession! Lead them like a shepherd, and carry them forever in your arms.

Get a (Spiritual) Life

Seeking first things first ...

The Words of Truth reveal that God is ...
___
___
___

The Words of Truth promise, warn, or teach me ...
___
___
___
___

To seek "first His kingdom and righteousness" today I will ...
___
___
___
___

The "other things" in my day that I must trust God for are ...
___
___
___
___

One of God's purposes that He has shown me in my day is ...
___
___
___
___

Day 28
Hold, Please

I love living in the modern age. There are so many innovations that enhance our lives. Microwave ovens. Electric pencil sharpeners. The Home Shopping Network. We live in a wondrous time. But of all the techno-miracles, telecommunication devices are the ones I appreciate the most.

Last year we decided to get a cellular phone for "emergencies." We purchased 150 minutes a month so I could call for help if I ran out of gas, had a flat, or came across a sale without my checkbook. It didn't take long, however, before I realized that my life was full of little "emergencies." I use my phone to make doctor's appointments, order Chinese, and check on the sitter. But what really runs up my minutes are those "emergency" calls to my friends. "Let's meet for coffee this morning." "Do you want to take the kids to the park this afternoon?" Now I have five hundred minutes, but since that's still just sixteen minutes a day, we save our longer discussions for the phone at home.

There, I can enjoy lingering over conversations with good friends without the threat of overcharges. Though we have limited time to be together, our relationships continue to flourish via fiber optics. You may wonder how I fit lengthy phone calls into my busy day. That's easy. I have a portable phone. I can bandage a scraped knee with one hand and hold the portable phone in the other. I can settle an argument with a snap and the "evil eye" while not missing a word of my friend's latest dilemma. Food preparation, discipline, kitchen disasters, and dogfights come and go, but the conversations carry on, because building those friendships is a priority.

The chaos is not just on my side of the receiver, either. A friend and I were recently talking about her grandmother's illness when her children interrupted her.

"Duke won't walk with us," I heard. Apparently, the kids had been walking the cat on a harness when he lay down and refused to go. "We dragged him for a little while, but he still won't get up," they laughed.

There was alarm in my friend's voice. "Oh no! The harness is choking him. Quick, get me the scissors." The cat was unconscious, and all the kids were talking at once.

"Mom, I can't find the scissors."

"Mom, why is Duke's tongue hanging out?"

Still, it didn't occur to either of us to hang up. Finally, the cat was cut loose and revived, and our conversation went on. (Duke, by the way, is fine.)

Similar incidents have replayed themselves during many phone conversations with close friends. Yet, because of our single-minded determination to maintain our relationships neither lack of time, nor tattling, nor gagging cat will detour us from our appointed calls.

It's surprising, then, that there is one Friend to whom I struggle to give my undivided attention. Even when I call on Him, staying focused is a challenge. The irony is, this is my wisest and most dependable Friend. This Friend is God. So why do I struggle so?

Get a (Spiritual) Life

Could it be the fault of my environment? Too much noise, too many problems, too little time? I want to say yes, but Jesus' life paints another picture. In the midst of a raging storm, with His friends in danger, He was praying. With a throng of people waiting to hear His life-giving message, He pulled away to pray. And in the garden, with soldiers on their way to arrest Him, Jesus would not be distracted from the time He needed to spend with His Father. It appears that distractions, responsibilities, and lack of time are not valid excuses for our inability to spend time with God. So how did He do it? How did Jesus stay awake and pray when He was exhausted? How did He put time with God first, even though the needs for His time were so great and the distractions so clamorous?

He lived as the psalmist lauded.

"Hear O Lord, and answer me ... for I am devoted to you. You are my God, save your servant who trusts in you ... for I call on you all day long. Bring joy to your servant, for to you O Lord, I lift up my soul.... Teach me your way, O Lord and I will walk in your truth; give me an undivided heart; I will glorify your name forever" (Ps 86, NIV).

An intimate prayer life with God begins with a heart devoted to God. Time with Him is worth unplugging the phone, hanging a "do not disturb" sign on the door, and giving Him our undivided hearts.

My purpose today is to phone home and have a long talk with my Father.

Psalm 17

O Lord, hear my plea for justice. Listen to my cry for help. Pay attention to my prayer, for it comes from an honest heart. Declare me innocent, for you know those who do right. You have tested my thoughts and examined my heart in the night. You have scrutinized me and found nothing amiss, for I am determined not to sin in what I say. I have followed your commands, which have kept me from going along with cruel and evil people. My steps have stayed on your path; I have not wavered from following you. I am praying to you because I know you will answer, O God. Bend down and listen as I pray. Show me your unfailing love in wonderful ways. You save with your strength those who seek refuge from their enemies. Guard me as the apple of your eye. Hide me in the shadow of your wings.... Because I have done what is right, I will see you. When I awake, I will be fully satisfied, for I will see you face to face.

Get a (Spiritual) Life

Seeking first things first ...

The Words of Truth reveal that God is ...

_____
_____
_____
_____

The Words of Truth promise, warn, or teach me ...

_____
_____
_____

To seek "first His kingdom and righteousness" today I will ...

_____
_____
_____
_____

The "other things" in my day that I must trust God for are ...

_____
_____
_____
_____

One of God's purposes that He has shown me in my day is ...

_____
_____
_____
_____

Day 29
The Greatest Story Never Told

Have I got a really great story to share with you! I knew immediately I would want to tell you all about it. It has everything a great story should have—humor, excitement, and a great ending. You would absolutely love it—if my daughter would let me tell you.

Since the story revolves around Hannah and her sensitive girl feelings, I knew I would have to ask her permission to share it. I was shocked when she said, "No way!"

"But honey," I pleaded, "It will make a great column."

With raised eyebrows, my nine-year-old daughter simply said, "No."

Generally, I don't ask the kids' consent when I include them in a story. The exception is if I think they might be embarrassed. I don't mean just run-of-the-mill embarrassment, like having your mom wipe a smudge off of your face with spit in public. That kind of humiliation is healthy. Unlike my friend, who recently shared with me that her full-time job is to keep from embarrassing her teenage daughter, my goal is to pay back just a little of the mortification my children have provided for me over the years. For instance, while back-to-school shopping, my ten-year-old son stopped me as I was jamming to the dressing room music.

"Mom," he said as he grabbed my swaying shoulder, "you're embarrassing me!"

This, coming from the boy who five minutes before was

Get a (Spiritual) Life

shooting enemy shoppers from inside the circular racks in the boys' department. This from the boy who puts straws up his nose in a restaurant and says, "Look, I'm a walrus." This from the same boy who set off the emergency exit alarm at the video store twice in one night. I'd say I was due a little retribution, and it's a rare thing to get it on this child. Bailey doesn't mind at all if I tell every detail of his life, just so long as I mention his name and often.

Chase, our oldest son, would much rather I wrote about his life than actually participate in it. That's why it's so much fun to torture him by working in his youth group and hanging out with his friends. The worst, though, according to my teenager, is when I give him advice in front of his pals, so I make sure to do that often. Payback, I remind him, for the hundreds of little ways he has brought a blush to my cheek over the years.

Hannah, though, sweet little Hannah, has a very short account with me. Except for that time when she was two and had a fit at the grocery store because I wouldn't buy her cookies, she has caused me no public humiliation. At age ten, going on thirty-five, she is kind and reasonable, and unlike her impulsive red-haired brother, she generally takes consequences into account before she decides to juggle tomatoes in the produce aisle.

When something embarrassing happens to her, there is no sense of justice attached. To tell a story, then, that would make her self-conscious could be done only with her permission, so I kept trying.

"Hannah, please let me tell about yesterday. It is such a fun story."

"No, Mom. It's my private life. I don't want you to write about it," she said definitively.

She was so determined, there was nothing left I could do—except, of course, bribe her. "What if I paid you for the rights to your story?"

"How much?"

"Five dollars."

"No way!" she said indignantly "I'll sell it for $100."

"No thanks," I told her. "I'll just wait and put it in next summer's book. By then you'll be older and won't care."

"Mom, I'll be eleven. I'll care."

I think at this point Hannah is banking on my flawed and very short memory. That, coupled with the fact that I want only the best for her, frees her from worry about having the issue brought up again.

Thank goodness we can have that same confidence in God. Though we have given Him countless reasons for a little retribution in our lives, by choice God has promised that He won't ever bring up our "most embarrassing moments."

"(God) has not punished us for all our sins, nor does he deal with us as we deserve.... He has removed our rebellious acts as far away from us as the east is from the west. The Lord is like a father to his children, tender and compassionate to those who fear him" (Ps 103:10-13).

The only story God wants to share about His children is how much they are loved.

My purpose today is to trust God with my deepest secrets and most embarrassing moments and also be trustworthy for others.

Psalm 103:1-18

Praise the Lord, I tell myself; with my whole heart, I will praise his holy name. Praise the Lord, I tell myself, and never forget the good things he does for me. He forgives all my sins and heals all my diseases. He ransoms me from death and surrounds me with love and tender mercies. He fills my life with good things. My youth is renewed like the eagle's! The Lord gives righteousness and justice to all who are treated unfairly. He revealed his character to Moses and his deeds to the people of Israel. The Lord is merciful and gracious; he is slow to get angry and full of unfailing love. He will not constantly accuse us, nor remain angry forever. He has not punished us for all our sins, nor does he deal with us as we deserve. For his unfailing love toward those who fear him is as great as the height of the heavens above the earth. He has removed our rebellious acts as far away from us as the east is from the west. The Lord is like a father to his children, tender and compassionate to those who fear him. For he understands how weak we are; he knows we are only dust. Our days on earth are like grass; like wildflowers, we bloom and die. The wind blows, and we are gone—as though we had never been here. But the love of the Lord remains forever with those who fear him. His salvation extends to the children's children of those who are faithful to his covenant, of those who obey his commandments!

Get a (Spiritual) Life

Seeking first things first ...

The Words of Truth reveal that God is ...
___
___
___
___

The Words of Truth promise, warn, or teach me ...
___
___
___

To seek "first His kingdom and righteousness" today I will ...
___
___
___
___

The "other things" in my day that I must trust God for are ...
___
___
___

One of God's purposes that He has shown me in my day is ...
___
___
___

Day 30
Who's on First?

I never dreamed my own child would one day be a champion. I would have called each of you right away, but I wanted to keep the phone line open in case the Wheaties people tried to call.

It all started in the summer, when thirteen boys were chosen to play on a baseball team that would represent our community in an attempt to win the honor of being called the best in the state. My Chase was one of those boys. That meant that while other families were enjoying their summer vacations, we remained in town for every practice. When it was time for the first game, we gave up prepaid tickets to Six Flags to return home early for the game, just to have it rained out.

Usually a rain-out is a welcome break, but not when the tournament is two hours away and the game is cancelled just as you're arriving. On several occasions the weather had the team all dressed up with no place to go, but they weren't discouraged. When they did play, our boys of summer were amazing. Winning thirteen of fourteen games, they prevailed over eighteen other teams to claim the state title.

Of all those games, the first in the state finals was the one that marked this team's character. Forty-eight hours after winning their second six-game series, and still more than a little tired, these thirteen boys stood in yet another ballpark, shaking hands with their final opponents. On this scorching summer afternoon, the best two out of three games would determine the victor.

During the entire first game, the heat and fatigue had our team playing catch-up. Just as we would tie the score the other team would widen their lead. As parents, we knew that if they lost, there was still a chance in the next game, but psychologically, a defeat would be hard to overcome.

The boys, on the other hand, weren't thinking about the next game at all. Facing the bottom of the last inning three runs behind, they had winning on their mind. With that goal (and one out and no men on base), Jamarcus stepped to the plate, smashing the first pitch over the center field fence for a homerun single. It was a glimmer of hope. We needed two more runs to take us to extra innings or three runs to win. They weren't giving up.

Chase was at the plate, and like any good mother I was pacing in the bleachers, praying he wouldn't strike out. The first pitch was a curve and Chase got caught looking. He fouled off the second pitch. The count was 0 and 2. I was a wreck. The pitcher wound up, let go, and threw an outside ball. I sweated it out, peeking through my fingers, as the count reached three balls and two strikes. Then came the wind up and the pitch and that beautiful sound of the crack of the bat! All eyes were on the ball. How many times had his flies been caught at the fence? The outfielder had his glove up but Chase's ball flew gloriously high over his head and out of the field. Back-to-back home runs!

Mayhem exploded in the bleachers and the dugout. A rally had been started and we could see victory. One hit after another loaded the bases until that final hit brought in the winning run. The rally didn't end until they had swept through the second game with a commanding win to earn the title State Champs.

As they received their trophy and accolades, it appeared that the championship had been won that night. The truth, however, was that the boys had earned that championship every day at practice when no one was watching. They had earned it with each of the hundreds of pitches that were thrown in fourteen games. They had earned it with every swing of the bat, every catch, and every slide in the games that came before the finals. They were champions in the end because all along the way they had shown championship behavior.

Holiness is exactly like that. No person, through one act of goodness, will find himself holding the Holiest Believer title. Holiness, that ability God gives us to act as He Himself would act, comes only through the everyday process of perseverance, consistency, and submission to God.

"As obedient children ... [be] like the Holy One who called you, be holy yourselves also in all [your] behavior; because it is written, 'You shall be holy, for I am holy'" (1 Pt 1:14-16).

As holiness becomes your way of life, you won't find yourself on a Wheaties box, but you'll be victorious nonetheless.

My purpose today is choose to behave as God would, moment by moment.

Psalm 25:8-21

The Lord is good and does what is right; he shows the proper path to those who go astray. He leads the humble in what is right, teaching them his way. The Lord leads with unfailing love and faithfulness all those who keep his covenant and obey his decrees. For the honor of your name, O Lord, forgive my many, many sins. Who are those who fear the Lord? He will show them the path they should choose. They will live in prosperity, and their children will inherit the Promised Land. Friendship with the Lord is reserved for those who fear him. With them he shares the secrets of his covenant. My eyes are always looking to the Lord for help, for he alone can rescue me from the traps of my enemies. Turn to me and have mercy on me, for I am alone and in deep distress. My problems go from bad to worse. Oh, save me from them all! Feel my pain and see my trouble. Forgive all my sins. See how many enemies I have, and how viciously they hate me! Protect me! Rescue my life from them! Do not let me be disgraced, for I trust in you. May integrity and honesty protect me, for I put my hope in you.

Get a (Spiritual) Life

Seeking first things first ...

The Words of Truth reveal that God is ...

_____
_____
_____
_____

The Words of Truth promise, warn, or teach me ...

_____
_____
_____
_____

To seek "first His kingdom and righteousness" today I will ...

_____
_____
_____

The "other things" in my day that I must trust God for are ...

_____
_____
_____
_____

One of God's purposes that He has shown me in my day is ...

_____
_____
_____

Day 31
Penalty for Early Withdrawal

You know what they say; it's never too early to start planning for retirement. Both Tony and I have plans for how we will spend our twilight years. Unfortunately, those plans are not the same.

I foresee having time to enjoy the simple pleasures of life together. I'll work in the rose garden. Tony will cultivate the perfect lawn. We might join a bowling league or perhaps take ballroom dancing. And with kids finally out of the house, we could redecorate our family home. I know there is life beyond washable wall paint and motorcycle wallpaper. We could buy furniture that doesn't have to withstand wrestling matches and ice cream spills. I could add throw pillows without the risk that they would actually be thrown.

Speaking of kids, there will be the grandchildren to consider. I envision my retirement years spent surrounded by small people calling me Nana or Grammy. If they live near us, we will of course want to spoil, I mean see, them often. We will be available to baby-sit at a moment's notice and wouldn't dream of missing a single childhood milestone. If they are far away, we'll spend our vacations traveling to see them. And the holidays will be one joyous reunion as our children and their families come back year after year to the home they know and love.

My husband sees things a little differently, however, starting with the homecoming. According to him, there won't be a home to come back to. At least not the one I've built my dreams around.

"Honey, as soon as the kids leave, I want to sell the house and move to a small place with an even smaller yard; one I can mow with a pair of scissors."

Sell? What about the holidays? What about the rose garden? What about the rooms for my grandchildren?

He had the answer to everything. "We won't have time for any of that. We are going to buy a motor home and travel most of the year. It will be great! We can visit golf courses all over the country."

Suddenly I knew why he had bought me, a nongolfer, a brand-new set of clubs for Christmas two years before. Well, you can lead the wife to clubs, but you can't make her swing. Unless one of us undergoes a drastic change of heart, retirement may not be an option for us.

Our situation seemed hopeless until we had dinner with a couple that was just nine months away from making that transition. Ken and Marilyn Foster were missionaries in Germany. We became friends fourteen years ago, when they were in our hometown on furlough. We were newlyweds and they offered to disciple us in a couples' small group. Since that time, we have watched God use them in incredible ways and have been privileged to pray for their ministry at an international school for missionary children.

The time had come, however, for them to consider their imminent retirement from oversees ministry, so they, too, were making plans. Theirs, though, didn't sound anything like my husband's or mine.

Get a (Spiritual) Life

Instead of planning for a well-deserved rest, they were searching for a new ministry challenge. And though grandchildren would certainly figure into their future, so, possibly, would taking aid and the gospel to disaster areas around the world. During retirement, their home would be as it had always been, a place decorated with love and hospitality toward friends and stranger alike.

To Ken and Marilyn retirement didn't mean more time for leisure, it meant more time for ministry. They didn't plan to walk quietly into the sunset. They planed to run with endurance all the way to the finish. That is the kind of retirement plan the Word of God endorses.

"(The righteous) are planted in the house of the Lord; they flourish in the courts of our God. They still bear fruit in old age; they are ever full of sap and green, to declare that the Lord is upright; He is my rock and there is no unrighteousness in Him" (Ps 92:13-15).

"Oh God, from my youth you have taught me and I still proclaim your wondrous deeds. So even in my old age and gray hairs, O God, do not forsake me until I proclaim your might to another generation, your power to all those to come" (Ps 71:17-18).

Tony and I agree that our own future plans still need a little tweaking. We will be starting from scratch and this time consulting the best Retirement Planner available.

My purpose today is to declare God's goodness, now and forever.

Psalm 150

Praise the Lord! Praise God in his heavenly dwelling; praise him in his mighty heaven! Praise him for his mighty works; praise his unequaled greatness! Praise him with a blast of the trumpet; praise him with the lyre and harp! Praise him with the tambourine and dancing; praise him with stringed instruments and flutes! Praise him with a clash of cymbals; praise him with loud clanging cymbals. Let everything that lives sing praises to the Lord! Praise the Lord!

Get a (Spiritual) Life

Seeking first things first ...

The Words of Truth reveal that God is ...

___

The Words of Truth promise, warn, or teach me ...

___

To seek "first His kingdom and righteousness" today I will ...

___

The "other things" in my day that I must trust God for are ...

___

One of God's purposes that He has shown me in my day is ...

___

Tomorrow Is Another Day

Congratulations! For an entire month you have experienced a spiritual life right smack dab in the middle of your real life. The great news is that you have created a routine of putting God's priorities first. It is amazing how all other things fall into place when we are faithful to follow where He leads. You may have had the same experience that I have in the past. Some things that I thought were so indispensable, so urgent, so pressing, God has revealed as things that needed to go altogether. By now you know that not everything in this world fits well into the spiritual life. As we walk more closely with God, He helps us weed out the urgent and keep the important. Always, though, the things we really need, He provides.

I pray that you will wake up tomorrow with the same sense of purpose that you have found in the last thirty-one days. As you continue to explore God's Word, to be encouraged by His promises, to develop a heart for His purposes, and to give Him first place in the moments of your day, may you discover a lifetime of tomorrows that add up to one amazing Spiritual Life.

Kim Wier
is the founder and president
of Engaging Women Ministries
*"Women Encouraging Women Through
Speaking, Writing, and Broadcasting"*
www.Engagingwomen.com

Kim is a newspaper humor columnist, co-host of
Engaging Women Radio Program, and a Christian
speaker and Bible teacher.

To schedule Kim to speak to your group, contact
Engaging Women Ministries at 936-560-4888.

If you would like to write to Kim, she invites you to
email to kim@engagingwomen.com

Other books by Kim Wier:

Are You Talking To Me?
Every Woman's Guide to Hearing From God

Redeeming the Season
*Simple Ideas for a Memorable and Meaningful
Christmas*

Coming Spring 2004
Redeeming the Season
Holy Halloween